# A BOY FROM BOTWOOD

BRYAN DAVIES | ANDREW TRAFICANTE

# A BOY FROM BOTWOOD

## Pte. A.W. Manuel,
## Royal Newfoundland Regiment,
## 1914–1919

DUNDURN
TORONTO

Cover image: February 1915, the Royal Newfoundland Regiment "Second Contingent" prepares to embark from St. John's to Britain, for eventual Mediterranean Expeditionary Force deployment in the Dardanelles (Gallipoli) campaign.
Printer: Webcom

**Library and Archives Canada Cataloguing in Publication**

Manuel, Arthur, 1895-1982, author
    A boy from Botwood : Pte. A.W. Manuel, Royal Newfoundland Regiment, 1914-1919 / edited by Bryan Davies, Andrew Traficante.

Includes bibliographical references and index.
Issued in print and electronic formats.
ISBN 978-1-4597-3671-9 (paperback).--ISBN 978-1-4597-3672-6
(pdf).--ISBN 978-1-4597-3673-3 (epub)

    1. Manuel, Arthur, 1895-1982. 2. Great Britain. Army. Newfoundland Regiment, 1st--Biography. 3. World War, 1914–1918--Personal narratives, Canadian. 4. Soldiers--Newfoundland and Labrador--Biography. 5. Newfoundland and Labrador--Biography. I. Traficante, Andrew, editor II. Davies, Bryan (Bryan T.), editor III. Title.

D640.M35 2017         940.4'8171         C2016-906272-4
                                        C2016-906273-2

1  2  3  4  5    21  20  19  18  17

We acknowledge the support of the **Canada Council for the Arts** and the **Ontario Arts Council** for our publishing program. We also acknowledge the financial support of the **Government of Ontario**, through the **Ontario Book Publishing Tax Credit** and the **Ontario Media Development Corporation**, and the **Government of Canada**.

VISIT US AT

dundurn.com  |  @dundurnpress  |  dundurnpress  |  dundurnpress

Dundurn
3 Church Street, Suite 500
Toronto, Ontario, Canada
M5E 1M2

*To Arthur W. Manuel, self-styled "common soldier," and his grandson
David Manuel, who preserved the Manuel manuscript*

# CONTENTS

# ACKNOWLEDGEMENTS

We are grateful for the kind advice and direction provided to us by Dr. Doug Delaney, Royal Military College of Canada (War Studies), as this work was in its early stages. We also thank the Royal Newfoundland Regiment Museum for its excellent guidance regarding the regimental history generally that assisted us in framing the Manuel story.

# INTRODUCTION

Why do Arthur Manuel's Great War experiences merit publication today, almost forty years after he made his late-in-life decision to tell his story? Manuel was an unheralded First World War veteran, a relatively anonymous Royal Newfoundland Regiment (RNR) private.[1] His impoverished rural Newfoundland village upbringing is depressing but unremarkable, given the early-twentieth-century life Manuel describes in his corner of Britain's "oldest and poorest colony." Large families, in an economy dominated by remote, imperious fishery and lumber "barons," often carved a bare subsistence living from a rugged, sometimes inhospitable, landscape. This was the shared experience for many young men who saw their August 1914 RNR enlistment as a way out.

Manuel's wartime service record in training and battle is equally undistinguished. He was never promoted. Formally and informally disciplined at various times for minor insubordinations, curfew violations, and misdemeanors, Manuel was not NCO (non-commissioned officer) material. His 1917 capture at Passchendaele and subsequent POW status until the Armistice was a longer imprisonment than endured by many others, but in a war where thousands were captured on both sides, this particular detail is not unique. On his May 1919 demobilization, Manuel leaves the regiment without regret, and shortly thereafter departs for Ontario — he never returned to Newfoundland for more than a few days at any time after 1921. He had little apparent contact with any fellow RNR First World War veterans during his long career as a hotel owner in faraway Windsor, Ontario. The most noticeable fact concerning Manuel's RNR service in the last sixty-six years of his life was his utter refusal to ever discuss it with anyone. War wounds, especially his badly scarred elbows, hips, and left foot were kept well covered. Questions from his children and later grandchildren regarding the old man's military experiences were bluntly dismissed by Manuel as being nobody's business — except his.

Manuel was a First World War RNR veteran — and his family knew very little else. No one dared to seek out any details. Other than his monthly Canadian veteran's pension cheques delivered in the mail, this taciturn man kept his wartime life secret. No medals were hidden in a drawer or displayed on his mantelpiece. No Gallipoli, Somme, or Passchendaele photographs were produced at his family gatherings, nor did Manuel permit any discussion concerning his military service to continue within his earshot. He did not belong to the Royal Canadian Legion, the country's official veterans' organization. Manuel is not known to have ever attended any of the annual November 11 commemoration ceremonies that have marked Remembrance Day in every Canadian city from 1920 onward. As his long life moved to its inevitable conclusion, Manuel did not merely systematically bury the Great War that he had survived — he seemingly obliterated it.

At age seventy-five, Manuel travelled alone to Beaumont-Hamel. He visited the terrible killing field, recalling how he survived the ill-fated July 1, 1916, RNR assault against German defences that signalled the beginning of the Battle of the Somme. Over eight hundred men had gone "over the top" — fewer than sixty answered roll call the next day. He made his own travel arrangements to reach France. No advance effort was made to contact his former regiment or to seek out anyone from his First World War life. His 1984 death in London, Ontario, was not publicly commemorated or noticed beyond the immediate Manuel family — just an old man's passing.

In our intensely digital age, where all personal information seems eventually accessible, it is difficult to imagine that facts concerning any First World War veteran's service and later life could not be ferreted out by anyone with an interest. Until years after Manuel's death, any research would have involved painstaking paper-file reviews and the co-operation of the subject to ensure the researcher was pointed in the right direction. Today, anyone can download Manuel's service record from the Veterans Affairs Canada website. It tells the bare bones account of his enlistment, training, deployment, service, capture, release, and demobilization. Brief mention is made of his German imprisonment, with cryptic references made to delays in his official POW registration, eligibility for Red Cross packages, and medical attention. The records kept by the passionate volunteers who maintain the RNR archives in St. John's are only slightly more informative. Manuel never discussed his POW experiences in any official pre-mobilization debriefing. He passed from the regiment's collective consciousness when he left for Ontario, never to return.

The proud RNR history spans four centuries, with battle honours won for the British Crown in service against Napoleon, in defence of the emerging Canada against the Americans in the War of 1812, and in its renowned Great War regimental "triple" — Gallipoli, the Somme, and Passchendaele.[2] Manuel is a previously anonymous piece in this honourable history. The dry official record would not prompt even the most diligent or passionate regimental researcher to make deeper inquiries regarding this man who left Newfoundland behind.

In 1980, at age eighty-four, what prompted Manuel to decide that he must now tell his Great War story? The Manuel family were only aware that the old man was infuriated over a Veterans Affairs decision to deny him a claim made for an additional monthly supplement. The precise dispute details are unknown.[3] Manuel did not need additional financial support; his retirement was reasonably comfortable — the proceeds of his Windsor hotel sale were sufficient for his modest late-in-life needs. Manuel's decision to purchase a dictation machine and commit his reminiscences to writing through the assistance of a local stenographer was only fully appreciated years after Manuel's death. As with his other First World War memories, Manuel did not discuss his personal history project with anyone, other than his stenographer. On receipt of her finished copy, Manuel put the work away, and it was only discovered by accident by his grandson in an unmarked box amongst other Manuel family effects in 2011. A nondescript shoebox, four hundred pages of single-spaced type, and sixty hours of tape are the raw materials from which *A Boy from Botwood* has been assembled.

Manuel's true motivation to tell his story after such a long, self-imposed silence, one marked only by his often belligerent refusal to answer any military service questions, will likely never be known. His Great War account is all the more compelling when set against this background. Manuel does not suggest his story is either a dispassionate dissertation or one that provides the reader with an infallible regimental history. He does not pretend to harbour any feelings except disdain, bordering at times on hatred, for the British military leadership whose decisions largely determined every RNR battle outcome. It is difficult at times to discern which elements of Manuel's descriptions of overall Allied war strategy are contemporary to his RNR service and which were driven by his later detailed, lifelong examination of how the war was actually conducted.

His extensive writings are a compendium of Manuel's personal experiences, overlaid with his later informal studies. Marxist-tinged views and socialist philosophy are each prominent, if secondary, themes providing powerful contradictions with the postwar life of this otherwise commercially successful hotel owner. *A Boy from Botwood* is the distillation of over sixty years of Manuel's wartime memories, filtered and re-filtered as his life moved on. These circumstances presented profound challenges for us, the custodians of his story, whose ambition was to ensure that Manuel's powerful, undimmed reminiscences were effectively fashioned into a cohesive, compelling narrative.

What resonates from every page of the original Manuel account is his passion and outright affection for his fellow common soldiers — Newfoundlanders, Allies, and Germans alike. Where Manuel has no love for the "brass hat" generals on either side, he shares the sentiment expressed by Erich Maria Remarque (author of *All Quiet on the Western Front*), and most otherwise-anonymous soldiers, that in every war, the true enemy is war itself.[4] Shaping Manuel's powerful personal sentiments into a single, focused work was the overarching *A Boy from Botwood* project objective.

The material is a treasure trove when understood as the ultimate legacy of this uncannily circumspect, observant First World War veteran. Lifelong personal reticence gives way to well-structured, detailed, and engaging accounts of Manuel's RNR and German POW experiences. His eye for detail is reinforced by the written word and sharply focused wherever apparent unfairness or inhumanity are encountered. Manuel's ready dry wit displayed on these pages is entirely at odds with the uncommunicative Great War veteran the Manuel family knew. Knowing Manuel's personal reputation, his raw reminiscence reads as if a long-fermenting, carefully distilled vintage has been uncorked — nuanced and intricate, often provocative, and rarely subdued.

Arthur Manuel would be a most unlikely, yet entirely attractive Great War memoirist if one ended the *Boy from Botwood* introduction here. Our deeper probing of his entire account ensured our profound appreciation for the sheer merit of Manuel's narrative — and his late-in-life commitment to "telling his story."[5] The bare official service record references to his Gallipoli, Somme, and Passchendaele experiences take on a different meaning when these are explained in his own words. He is one of the few 1914 Newfoundland volunteers to have served and survived the entire war. The seventeen months Manuel spent in POW captivity acquires fresh historical lustre when the reader appreciates Manuel is the *only* North American First World War prisoner-soldier to have committed his story for posterity in such graphic detail. The account of his dramatic late-1917 escape from an unofficial, but all too real, German POW slave camp, his recapture, and the vicious assault he later experienced at the hand of the angry, vengeful POW camp commandant — who cut off part of Manuel's left foot with an axe — is like no other, and every event has now been corroborated by regimental reports and Canadian military archival materials, supplemented by original German POW and hospital records.

*A Boy from Botwood* is at once a personal history, a Great War indictment, an unvarnished reminiscence, and — although its author may never have admitted it — an endearingly warm Manuel tribute. These reminiscences — by a man who never sought recognition in a life so acutely shaped by war and its misery — confirm the author's enduring faith in the human spirit as an irrepressible force for good. Perhaps Manuel's message is more compelling today for his not having previously shared it with anyone else.

The chapters we present in this work are Manuel's words alone, edited only to ensure greater clarity and chronological certainty. Manuel assembled his various memories with the war as their connective thread. After reading the four hundred pages of text and listening to the audiotapes, it became clear to us that Manuel recalled his life story in pieces. Where an incident that occurred during combat is described, the narrative might shift quickly to those still-powerful, pervasive POW camp memories. As often, the RNR front-line experiences are peppered with recollections of Manuel's Botwood youth or juxtaposed against a recent conversation with his London, Ontario, neighbours. Our supporting text is positioned at various points in the original narrative to supplement Manuel's remarkable, incisive voice, one that reflects the entire span of our collective human experience, where hope and sorrow, affection and fear, compassion and hatred remain spontaneous, unfiltered, and resolutely real.

Bryan Davies and Andrew Traficante

# CHAPTER ONE

## BOTWOOD, 1908

When I had reached what my teacher said would be the equivalent of the seventh grade in a regular public school, my poor dear old father, with tears in his eyes and his voice filled with emotion, broke the bad news he could no longer afford to pay any further tuition fees. I was twelve years old at the time, but I sobbed myself to sleep that night.

Next day I began work in a sawmill, where I received the magnificent sum of fifty cents — not fifty cents an hour, but fifty cents a day. The workdays were ten hours long in those days and included Saturdays. We worked a full sixty hours each and every week, fifty-two weeks a year. Christmas and Good Friday were the only two so-called holidays, but we weren't paid for either.

My first job at the mill was carrying wet and heavy water-soaked lumber from the saws to the drying yard, two hundred feet away or more. It was work that in most civilized countries was performed only by trucks and horses. When I had been there for about a year or so, one of the owners came over from England to look the place over. I suppose that because of my age, he came out to where I was stacking the lumber and asked me a whole lot of questions. He wanted to know whether or not I had attended school and for how long; how many brothers and sisters I had; what kind of work my father did for a living; and if I intended to remain on the Island, or to migrate to the U.S.A. or Canada, as most of the young Newfoundland people were doing.

He took both my hands in his, turned them palms up, and began prodding at them with his thumb, but they were so thoroughly and deeply calloused from the friction of so many planks sliding through my hands day after day that the prodding could barely be felt.

"Why don't you wear gloves?" he inquired. "Because I can't afford them," I replied. "Oh yes, that is so," he said, "and something must be done about it. I have been talking with your foreman and he tells me that you are a very hard and conscientious worker, so I am going to ask the manager to increase your salary."

Oh boy, for the next couple of weeks, I was walking on air with my head in the clouds. But when payday came at the end of the month and I was told by the big, fat, pot-bellied Scandinavian manager that Mr. Crowe (the owner) had only recommended a ten-cent per day raise in my wages and in future I would be paid the grand total of sixty cents per day, I could not believe my ears. Whether he was lying or not, I had no way of knowing. In any case, there was nothing I could do about it as there were plenty of others, both men and boys, waiting to take the job if I dared to make a complaint.

After two years, I was sent by the mill bosses to mine some limestone for the Grand Falls Paper Company.[1] The father of the woman I boarded with during my six weeks stay there was ninety-three years old — he had never seen a genuine banknote of any description prior to his eighty-fourth birthday. He told me that for his entire catch of fish during the year prior to his retirement, he was paid a mere one dollar per quintal.[2] Therefore, he received less than one cent per pound for the very same kind of sun-cured codfish that I have paid as much as $3.98 per pound for today. We poor old Newfies, as the mainlanders call us, always get the small end of the stick and more often than not, the dirty end as well.

There were no modern, quick, frozen-fish plants in those days, where an independent fisherman could sell and be paid for his quota of fish on the day it was caught. It took a whole summer, or the better part of one, to prepare fish for the market. From catching, cleaning, and curing the fish, a monotonous, back-breaking routine was followed day after day until the entire summer catch had been processed and made ready for market. In the meantime, the poor individual family fisherman was required to buy everything he needed in the line of food, clothing, and fishing supplies, from the multi-millionaire merchants who bought his fish. Like the poor, hard-working miners and lumber mill men, he was robbed on both counts.

Our life was relentlessly hard, whether a family lived from the land, the woods, the mines, or the sea. In a way it prepared me for starvation and near-death when I was a prisoner of war. Sharing with others the little I had was neither new nor unusual. To borrow, loan, or give outright had been, for a high percentage of the people belonging to England's oldest, poorest, and most neglected colony, a regular and recognized way of life. Down through the centuries, our neighbours had always been our one and only insurance (as we were theirs) against both hunger and disaster. None of our people ever felt embarrassed or inferior when circumstances beyond our control compelled us to seek help from our neighbours. It was an accepted and confirmed way of life at that time, and in all probability, in the far northern section of Newfoundland where I was born, it still is to some extent. This would be particularly so during the long winter months when, due to the ice and stormy weather, ships (still the only means of transportation to some of the northern towns) were forced to remain in port.

In my childhood days back home, if one of the villagers shot a moose, caribou, or any other kind of game, he never embarrassed his neighbours by asking if they wanted some. He simply cut it up into equal portions and delivered it to the various homes as though they had all bought and paid for it. In a sense, they had, for next time it would be their turn to keep the account sheet in balance.

While no community of people were ever more dependent on each other than were those of the little outports where I was born and grew up, the words *dole, relief, welfare,* or any kind of government handout as it is generally understood today, were altogether foreign and totally without meaning to our people. Admittedly, we were poor and by today's standard of living, we would be considered very poor indeed. Nevertheless, nobody ever went hungry (at least not for long) and we prided ourselves on being one of the nation's most free and independent people.[3]

Despite our lack of riches and luxury, we were content to make do with what we had. I would say that it was just another case of "Where ignorance is bliss, 'tis folly to be wise." In other words, what one has never had, one has never missed. Perhaps our biggest and most important consolation was the fact that we were all in the same boat together. There were no Joneses to keep up to, nor to envy. Although without choice, we were an absolute 100 percent classless society — not that I would recommend it for others, or that I would prefer to live it all over again myself.

Speaking of the devil — our newspaper boy just handed me the morning paper, and one of the headlines on the front page reads, "A family of four with an income of less than seventeen thousand is living on or below the poverty line." *Good God,* I thought, *that is as much or more than my dear old father made during his entire lifetime of eighty-eight years, and he fathered a family of twelve ...*[4]

———

These piecemeal Botwood recollections are ones that Manuel regularly intersperses among his Great War accounts. These memories reveal the practical reasons why he was quick to enlist with the RNR when war was declared in August 1914. Manuel had worked in a variety of difficult, often dangerous jobs for very little pay. The army promised a uniform, regular meals, better pay, and adventure — powerful lures for the rural and outport Newfoundlanders for whom the description *hardscrabble* would be appreciated as an understatement. And, after all, the British political leadership and their Newfoundland representatives assured the newly enlisted colonials that the war would be over by Christmas. The ceaseless, hard-grinding Botwood life could be suspended, if only for a time. It would be a shame to miss the fun.

# CHAPTER TWO

## ST. JOHN'S, AUGUST 1914

For Manuel and many other Newfoundlanders who saw the war as an opportunity for something better, and a respite from a hard life, the August 1914 RNR[1] enlistment at the St. John's regimental headquarters was quick and uncomplicated. Although not part of the celebrated "First 500" to join the regiment as soon as the call for volunteers went out,[2] Manuel's regimental number — 867 — confirms his early volunteer status. Manuel's account of those early days is at once wistful, humorous, and tinged by the dark memories that colour his entire reminiscence. The painfully amateurish but passionate Newfoundland response to their British motherland's call to arms starkly frames Manuel's far more searing front-line combat accounts of Gallipoli, the Somme, and Passchendaele.

Manuel mentions his RNR training at various points in his original, unedited narrative. The best and most evocative account flows from a memory triggered as he recalled life in the Bavaria prison camp near war's end. Manuel recounts how he was first captured at Passchendaele in May 1917, badly wounded and lying in a shell crater with three dead German soldiers, and what he did to save himself from bleeding to death. At the Bavarian camp, he watched young German soldiers training in an adjacent parade square and performing drills that prompted comparisons with those he learned in his early military career.

———

I am getting to be a very old man and much of the misery of those terrifying years has dimmed and faded, but the picture of those three dead German soldiers — and especially so the youth whose bayonet I borrowed to tighten the tourniquet on my arm — has always remained vividly clear and regretfully sad. As I sat there watching the various drills and manoeuvres, I frequently noticed that one of the older drill sergeants in charge of the new recruits appeared to frown or scowl every time he looked in my direction, as though he resented my being there.

So one afternoon, when the camp commandant stopped on the way to his office to ask me how my foot was coming along,[3] I asked him if he thought the sergeant minded my sitting there to watch them drill. "Certainly not," he said, "but if it will make you feel more comfortable, I will ask him." I have no idea of just what the commandant said to him, but from that day on, the old drill sergeant was as friendly as the rules permitted.

The following afternoon when I got there, I saw a very old adjustable-type deck chair leaning against the outside of the barbed wire enclosure. A short time later, when the squads being drilled were halted for a rest period, the sergeant and one of his new recruits, a lad who did not appear to be a day over sixteen, came over. The recruit climbed halfway up the outside of the fence. The sergeant handed him up the chair and he passed it down on the inside to me. Speaking in broken but quite understandable English, he said, "My sergeant would very much like for you to have this chair instead of sitting on that hard, cold stone, and he wishes me to say that he is very sorry for being so rude to you, but he thought that you were one of those proud professional English soldiers who came each day only to watch the awkwardness of his new men in training so that you could entertain your comrades at night by telling them what a dumb bunch of soldiers we are. After talking it over with your camp commandant, he is satisfied that this is not so, and he wishes me to say that you are quite welcome to come and watch as often as you please …"

I wished that I could have assured that old German drill sergeant of the far superior type of training his recruits were receiving compared to the kind we got when we first enlisted, but that would have taken far too long. Moreover, the humour would have gotten lost in the translation. If it had been possible for that old professional soldier to have seen our boys trying to manoeuvre themselves into some kind of military formation, he would still be laughing.

To begin with, there was no one where we enlisted in St. John's who knew how to train us, except a small church group — I think they called themselves the Methodist Boys' Brigade. The instructor of my squad had once been a boy scout and the sum total of his knowledge in military matters was his ability to rub a couple of sticks together and start a fire. Personally, I had never seen a soldier, professional or otherwise, and if I had known what I was letting myself in for, I probably never would have.

It did not matter too much about our two left feet, or whether we were in or out of step during the four or five weeks that we were billeted at St. John's. There were few if any in that town at that time with sufficient knowledge of military procedures to qualify them as critics, although I did hear of one lady who remarked to a neighbour after we had marched past her home on Gower Street that almost everyone except George had been out of step. George, of course, was her son. It was not so all-important to look like real or well-trained soldiers to people who had seldom (if ever) seen any, and we could parade up and down and all around town in ignorant bliss. It was a very different situation, however, when we arrived in Scotland and took over the garrison of Edinburgh Castle from one of the most famous regiments in the British Empire.

Even now, seventy years later, I can still feel a kind of self-consciousness when I think back and try to visualize just what we must have looked like to a crack regiment of professional soldiers capable of performing all of the most complex military manoeuvres and ceremonial parades with absolute precision. They stood and watched us straggle in over that historical esplanade, out of step and out of line, like busloads of sightseeing tourists. But to their eternal credit, not one of them cracked a smile or made a comment — at least not one that we could see or overhear. Later, when we had become better acquainted, we took plenty of good-natured ribbing.

A month or so after our arrival there, I met a member of that famous regiment in a downtown hotel. He invited me to his home, and after we had got to know each other fairly well, he jokingly related some of the humorous cracks and remarks made by some of his roommates at their barracks on the night following our arrival at the castle, such as, "My God,

Jock, England must already be scraping the bottom of the barrel!" "That outfit looks as though it could be Britain's 'last hope'!" and "Well, I must say — if those ladies represent the army, thank God we still have the navy!"

But, despite our ignorance of military matters and procedures, it did not take too long for those old professional army instructors to mould us into a reasonable facsimile of real soldiers. If any member of that famous regiment who saw us when we marched into the castle happened to be there three months later to see us when we marched out for the very last time, I feel sure he would have changed his mind about our being Britain's last hope.

There was one thing that the most of us could do and do well — we could shoot, and shoot straight. Our musketry instructors never grew tired of complimenting us on our marksmanship or bragging about it to the other units on all of our trips to the rifle range. There was of course a reason for our more accurate marksmanship — for some of us not a very happy one. Back home, many of us were dependent on the fish hook and rifle for our livelihood, and frequently, when we failed to shoot straight, we went short of food. There appears to be less necessity for that kind of hunting and killing in recent years, for which I am pleased and thankful. I have always hated to shoot or kill any living creature — including and above all, my fellow human beings — nor have I ever owned or used any kind of gun since the war ended. Nevertheless, a good rifleman was more important in France and the Dardanelles than were any number of ceremonial parades or precision drills.

Scotland is a most beautiful country and its Edinburgh capital is not only picturesque and beautiful, it is magnificent. All of our Newfoundland boys who got their early training there would readily agree that no people in all the earth are more kind, considerate, and generous than the Scots. They invited us to their homes, churches, and theatres, wined and dined us, and while serving in France and the Dardanelles, we received letters of cheer and good wishes together with many food and comfort parcels, which I am sure some of them could ill afford. Any of us fortunate enough to obtain hospital leave during our convalescence from wounds never failed to hightail it back up to Scotland, where we could be sure of enjoying every last minute of our very brief furlough with our wonderful warm-hearted friends.

Edinburgh Castle sits high on a hill in the centre of the old city. The townspeople refer to it as "Castle Rock." If there had been any other way out of the castle except through the main gate, some of our boys would have found it. It would have saved them much trouble hiding underneath the bottoms of coal carts and garbage wagons, sliding down the outside of the castle ramparts on lengths of historical hangman's rope (borrowed without permission from the castle museum), plus many other ingenious plots and schemes thought up when, for one reason or another, they could not obtain a pass. You see, finding their way downtown to keep their pre-arranged dates was a must.

We worked very hard at the castle and so did the men who drilled and converted us into as good a fighting unit as time permitted. It was not all work and sweat, however. It had its lighter sides, some of which were rather amusing, although the laughs were usually at our expense. Our first and biggest blooper occurred shortly after taking over guard duty.

The entrance to the castle at that time was guarded by a small squad of soldiers, but only one man stood watch as sentry at the gate — the others retired to the guard house located just inside the entrance, to await their turn. One of the duties of the sentry standing watch was to salute all commissioned officers, ranking up to and including colonels, by coming to attention and passing his right hand over to the butt of his rifle, which he carried at a sloping angle on his left shoulder. All ranks above that of colonel, including all the various ranks of generals, are entitled to the "present-arms" salute.

When one or more of those brass hats makes an appearance, the sentry must immediately call out all the other members of the guard by shouting loud and clear, "Guard turn out!" Then, as the general approaches the entrance, the sentry gives the command to present arms. The whole guard, including the sentry, snaps briskly to attention, bringing their rifles to the present-arms position and holding them so until the general has passed through. Should the sentry fail to make the proper identification, there is no time left to make a correction after the guard has been called out. Our boys had, of course, been given all of this information prior to their assignment, but the sentry on duty at this particular time had never even seen a general and had little or no idea of what one looked like.

Although the sentry was far from being an expert regarding the insignias and uniforms of high-ranking officers, he was nevertheless a very alert and observant sentinel. When he saw a most distinguished looking gentleman coming up the castle esplanade — all decked out with much gold braid on the collar and sleeves of his tunic, bright red bands around his cap and down each leg of his trousers, rows of ribbons across his chest — there was no doubt whatever in his mind that a man dressed in so much elaborate regalia must be at least a general (perhaps even a field marshal).

The general appeared to quicken his step as he neared the entrance, and the sentry suspected that he may be trying to catch him off guard, or lax in his duty. Well, he would show this "brass hat" whether he was lax in his duty or not. Yelling with all his lung power, he ordered the guard to turn out; then with another mighty blast as the general came through the portal, he gave the command to present arms, which appeared to scare the approaching man to death.

And so this is how it came about that one of Edinburgh's humble but well-decorated hotel porters was suddenly — and without his knowledge or consent — promoted to the rank of a full general in His Majesty's Armed Forces and accorded full military honours in keeping with his high rank and office.

It took quite some time to live that one down. On parade downtown, or during a route march through the countryside, we were bound to meet or pass units of Scottish troops who seldom missed an opportunity for a little good-natured ribbing. First, one of their number would call out to other members of his company and pose the question, "Who presented arms to the hotel porter?" Then a chorus of voices in that deep Scots brogue would respond, "Hoot-mon! That was the Newfoundland ladies from across the big loch!" Sometimes, they would content themselves by simply inquiring about the general's health, or if "General Porter" was still with us.

It was, of course, all in good-natured fun and not meant to sting, but some of our more sensitive boys did take exception to so much razzing, and one night downtown, perhaps after both sides had indulged in a drop too much of that good Scotch whisky, a little blood was spilled. No serious or lasting harm was done and the incident was soon forgotten.

Although the castle was beautiful, picturesque, and one of the most historical and interesting structures to visit in the whole of Britain, or in any other country, it was not at all a nice place to live. The Scotch mist and the cold winds blowing in from the North Sea tended to keep our old stone sleeping quarters continually damp, cold, and very uncomfortable. The few scuttles of coal we were allowed each week were never enough to warm the place up, not even when we used up the whole week's issue in just one night (which we usually did). But for the wonderful, warm-hearted friends we had made in the city, we would have been quite willing and happy to leave the castle at any time.

We were much more comfortable and suffered far less from colds when we moved from the castle to Stobs Camp, where we slept under canvas in bell-shaped army tents. Stobs Camp,[4] located about three miles from the lovely town of Hawick and within ten or twelve miles of the English border, was more or less open country with beautiful meadows and well-cultivated fields. Owing to the shortage of tents, we were much overcrowded, sleeping ten to twelve in a tent that was meant only for eight. When the weather was good, which was most of the time during our stay there, some of us took our blanket and damp-proof ground sheet outside and slept in the open field.

The bugler — the guy who someone was always threatening to murder — woke us up every morning at 5:30. A day's route march was seldom less than fifteen miles and frequently as much as twenty, depending on who got tired first — the captain or his horse. Despite all the long, tiresome marches, drills, and manoeuvres, there were very few boys who did not walk an extra six miles each evening, either to keep or to make dates with some of Scotland's most beautiful young women.

Hawick, with a population of about sixteen thousand, was a most beautiful town. It had several fabric and cloth manufacturing mills, which even in peacetime employed far more women than men. When the war came, just about every young man who was physically fit joined the forces and marched away, leaving behind a town full of beautiful young women ... and a soldier's paradise. The unmarried men in our regiment would regularly receive "my dearest" letters from either Hawick or Edinburgh after we arrived in the Dardanelles — and some of the more philandering-type boys were receiving some from both.

Several hundred new boys from home joined us shortly after our arrival at Stobs Camp, all of whom would remain in Scotland for further training and rejoin us later (what was left of us), as reinforcements — a reserve unit — to fill the gaps and keep our front-line battalion up to full strength as the need arose. We were well aware now that, since sufficient reserves had arrived to take care of any initial casualties, it would not be long until we were on our way to the front. We had, however, taken it for granted that we would be going to France and were very much surprised a few weeks later at Aldershot, when informed by Secretary of [State for] War Lord Kitchener, that within a day or two, we would be on our way to the Dardanelles to fight the Turks.

Shortly after the company of new men from home joined us at Stobs Camp, one of their number — a big, tall, husky lad from one of our far northern Newfoundland outports — was detailed for guard duty and posted at one of the bridges about midway between camp and town. Like me, he had never seen any professional soldiers (or any other kind for that matter) prior to enlisting. There was nothing important or strategic about the bridge — at least not in a military sense. It was just a simple wood structure over a railway line. The idea was not so much to protect the bridge as it was to help in the training of new recruits.

Sometime during the night or early morning, one of those newly commissioned, self-important English second lieutenants, on his way back to camp after a night on the town, came over the bridge, and after returning the new sentry's salute, stopped to chat awhile. He complimented the new man on his very clean and well-cared-for rifle and asked if he might have a closer look. Thinking the young officer just wanted to be friendly, the inexperienced man handed over the rifle, which, of course, he should not have done. A soldier on duty must never give up his rifle to anyone — not even to a general.

Once in possession of the rifle, the highly self-esteemed lieutenant stuck its muzzle in the poor bloody recruit's chest and began to browbeat him for giving it up. Now well aware of his mistake in parting with his rifle, the big fellow stood and took all of the miserable subaltern's abuse in complete submission. However, when informed by his tormenter that he was not a British officer, but a disguised German spy, the sentry took him at his word and treated him accordingly. Quickly grabbing the rifle away with one hand, he punched the officer so hard in the face with the other closed fist that, in addition to being hospitalized for several weeks with a broken jaw, much dental work would be required before the would-be future general could again rejoin his fellow officers at the camp.

The story soon spread far and wide and got to be a very interesting and amusing topic of conversation both in camp and out. This time, however, nobody in the other units attempted to rib any of our boys about the incident, nor did any outside officer ever again ask if he might take a look at one of our rifles. A considerable number of these young, newly commissioned officers belonging to the privileged class, and, in most cases, just out of college, spent the major part of their off-duty time trying to make their less fortunate countrymen feel humble and inferior. They actually worked overtime attempting to prove their superiority and seldom, if ever, missed an opportunity to plague and humiliate the common private volunteer, or what most of them referred to as the "enlisted men."

The trick of asking to see a man's rifle was just one of the many mean and irritating methods they practised in order to display their rank and to make the common enlisted man feel ill at ease and uncomfortable. In the evenings, they walked the streets by the hour for the sole purpose of having the enlisted men salute them, and regardless of how busy the streets were, if a man missed seeing and saluting one of those arrogant upstarts, or failed to salute in the prescribed manner and in accordance with what was termed the King's Rules, he was in trouble. Frequently, after a man had saluted one of these hams, the big show-off would walk up or down the street a block or two, then turn round and walk all the way back, so that the poor bloody enlisted man must salute him all over again.

Some of those contemptible little men whose uniform gave them the authority to inflict indignities on others would stop a private soldier on the street and look him over from head to foot as if he was just another article of merchandise that they were about to purchase. Should a button of his uniform be loose or unfastened, his shoes not mirror-bright, or his cap not precisely at the prescribed regulation angle, his name and number would be taken down and a full report of this "shocking and dastardly crime" would be mailed in to his regimental headquarters. A few days later, the poor soldier would be ordered up for trial and perhaps sentenced to seven days CB ("confined to barracks"), depending on the knowledge and to what extent his own CO [commanding officer] was prejudiced, pro or con.

The fact that the self-important sub-lieutenant asked to see the new guard's rifle, and boasted of being a German spy after he got it, put the guard well within his rights to use any means available to him in order to get it back. Therefore, his only crime was in parting with his rifle, which, being a new man with little or no military training, would have carried very little weight in the case of a court martial. On the other hand, if the young officer had said nothing about being a German spy and the sentry had struck him, the charge would have been a most serious one indeed.

All officers had the right to check on outside guards and patrols if they cared to do so, but most common-sense officers, particularly those promoted from the ranks, found more interesting things to do during their off-duty evenings. Apparently, in this case, the senior officers of both regiments considered it best for all concerned to have the whole unpleasant incident hushed up and forgotten about as soon as possible. For that reason, no formal charge was ever made against the new guard — and to the many other high-spirited souls (especially so to those who had been subjected to similar humiliations and indignities), he soon got to be known as the most popular man at the camp.

Strangely enough, just a few months later, during the near-to-unbearable monotony and misery of the Dardanelles, one could frequently overhear some of those very same boys reminiscing about the good old days back in Scotland and how when they were AWOL (absent without official leave), they were obliged to match wits by playing that old familiar game of "hide and seek" with so many of those crafty little one-pip sub-lieutenants in order to keep themselves out of the pokey.

It seems those big little men, who took themselves so seriously, had lost all interest in us after we left for the battlefront. Not one of them ever came to check as to whether or not we were out there in no man's land with loose or unfastened buttons on our tunics or if our shoes were properly shined and our caps at the prescribed angle and in accordance with the King's Rules. Nor did any of them ever come and ask if they could take a look at our rifles. Then there were the men at the other end of the officer scale — the top generals. They never came to visit us either but, of course, they had a good reason for not coming. They felt it necessary to remain anywhere from ten to fifty miles beyond the danger zone, in order to direct us in the fighting.

During the many beautiful sunny afternoons that I sat in that old, worn, and tattered deck chair and watched the hundreds and thousands of those poor unfortunate German boys being prepared for the slaughter (most of them under nineteen years old and some less than seventeen), I frequently thought back to our last and final two weeks' training at Aldershot, prior to embarking for Egypt and the Dardanelles.

Aldershot, which was England's biggest and most important military depot, must have had at least a quarter of a million troops there at that time, half (perhaps more) of which were new recruits. In comparing the two altogether different methods of training, it would be difficult to conceive that both sides were being trained for the same purpose — the purpose of fighting and killing each other in the same war. Now, I could readily see and understand why our casualties on the British sector of the Western Front were two and a half times greater than the Germans. For every thousand German soldiers we killed, they killed twenty-five hundred of ours. That is supposed to be the official count, but some members of the government, including Mr. Churchill, put the ratio as high as three to one in Germany's favour. During the Battle of the Somme, it was many times higher than that.

In my view and that of all the other prisoners who watched each day, the German method was at least a whole generation ahead of the British in both defensive and offensive tactics. Each new German recruit was issued with a book of instructions, including a manual of arms, listing a complete outline of all of the many drills and manoeuvres that he would be taught to perform, plus the many and various types of weapons that he would be trained to operate. There was never any browbeating, tongue-lashing, or yelling of obscenities at a new recruit when he had made a mistake, as was so often the case at Aldershot.

After about forty minutes of brisk drills and manoeuvres, twenty minutes or so would be spent as a rest and study period. The German officers and drill sergeants would sit down and talk over with the new recruits any errors they had made. The recruits would write them down, and during the many days that I sat and watched, I never saw any one recruit make the same mistake a second time. There was far more comradeship, friendliness, and goodwill between German officers and their men. If a new man made a wrong turn or was out of step, the officer in charge would bring the platoon or company to a halt, walk over to the man at fault, and in a friendly manner explain to him where he had gone wrong and how best to correct it. In comparison, the method of training new recruits at Aldershot was crude, clumsy, and tactless.

I never did see one of those loud-mouthed instructors at Aldershot sit down or stop and discuss with his men the kind of drills or manoeuvres that they were about to take part in. The recruits were lined up one behind the other (or, to use the military phrase, two-deep), and from that position, orders and commands were shouted and barked at them as if the men were cattle being driven to the slaughterhouse. When a boy made a mistake, he was tongue-lashed, ridiculed, and made to appear awkward and ridiculous in front of his friends and comrades.

Much of the language used by some of those ignorant old men at Aldershot is unprintable, although there was never anything new or original about their coarse, sarcastic rebukes — just a lot of dirty catch phrases and vulgar slogans, which some of their ancestors had used centuries before. So many thousands of those young Englishmen and teenage boys who, when war came, had voluntarily given up good jobs, schools, and comfortable homes to fight for their country were treated little or no better than slaves or chattels by some of those loud and dirty-minded old men.

I recall one of those old walrus-style-moustached instructors who kept shouting at one of the new recruits to keep his legs in a certain position during bayonet practice. Finally, he yelled, "No, no, no damn it, not that way! Apart, apart! Keep your legs apart, like your sister would if she was about to be loved!" But *loved* was not the word he used. Dirty-minded, foul-mouthed old men …

———

Manuel conveys a deeply engrained sense of fairness and egalitarianism in his account of the RNR training that spans initial recruitment, Edinburgh, Stobs, and Aldershot. One senses in reading it that Manuel's views concerning how people ought to treat one another were fully formed in rural Botwood. His training, and the war, wounds, and capture only reinforced Manuel's resolute world view.

# CHAPTER THREE

## GALLIPOLI, 1915

The RNR was the only North American military unit to see action in the Dardanelles campaign, with the Battle of Gallipoli its most prominent engagement. Far from achieving First Sea Lord of the Admiralty Winston Churchill's objective, where Allied invaders would strike at the "soft underbelly of Europe" and bring the war to a quick end, Gallipoli was an operational disaster. The British Expeditionary Force's (BEF) April 1915 landing was the first to feature the RNR, Australian, and New Zealand "colonial" forces in prominent roles.

The ensuing nasty eight-month stalemate, with BEF units unable to break out from their beachhead against determined Turkish opposition, is the backdrop against which Manuel recalls his Gallipoli experience. British officers had assured the men they would be facing a bloodthirsty and cruel Turkish enemy. Such images of a dishonourable enemy were soon proven false for Manuel, who describes his deep respect for the formidable Turkish soldiers. It is the ever-present fear of death, combined with filth, disease, and privation, that colours every Manuel reminiscence of Gallipoli.

———

At the end of our one-year service in 1915, every man in our whole battalion became free to do as he pleased. He could accept his discharge and return home to his family and friends, or he could volunteer to re-enlist and serve for the duration of the war. To the best of my knowledge, not one man or boy in our battalion of well over a thousand decided on taking his discharge, though the longing for home, freedom, and safety must have been overwhelming — particularly so for some of the very young teenagers who had lied successfully about their age in order to be accepted.

But instead of choosing home, freedom, safety, and loved ones, which they had every right to do, and being well aware that they could be signing their own death warrants, every last man and boy in the entire battalion volunteered to re-enlist for a second term and for the duration of the war. Unfortunately, close to half of those who signed did not live to come home....

Our regiment first saw action a few weeks after being attached to the British Mediterranean expeditionary forces at Cairo, Egypt, in the summer of 1915, from where we later embarked for Gallipoli and the Dardanelles to face and fight some of the world's most courageous and enduring soldiers, better known to our boys as the "Terrible Turks." I am convinced that as guerilla-type fighters or individual snipers and sharp-shooters, the Turkish soldiers have few if any equals. Most of the time, it was like trying to fight an army of ghosts, for although few of them were ever seen except in open battle, we could feel and sense their presence everywhere around and about us.

Every one of our boys killed by snipers in the Dardanelles was shot through the head. In most cases, if they had heeded the advice of their more careful and cautious comrades to keep their heads down and under cover, they would have been spared (at least from snipers). How often I had heard one boy warn another that he was raising his head too often and keeping it up too long, but there were always the few who felt that to act overcautious was to appear less courageous. For the majority of us, it was just a case of good old-fashioned horse sense.

The very patient Turkish sniper, well aware that he would not be given a second chance to shoot at the same target, bided his time. It seemed that he would rather not shoot at all than shoot and take a chance of missing his target. If one or more of them observed any of us working on a trench or building up a parapet, they did not blaze away at the first man who showed his head above ground for a second or two, as both the British and Germans were more apt to do. They tended to hold their fire, allowing us ample time to think that we were not being observed. Sometimes they seemed to understand just how we would react to certain situations, as well or even better than we did ourselves. They also knew that there were some among us who were more daring and foolhardy than others and if they waited long enough, their patience would be rewarded.

Most of the boys in our regiment could smell and sense danger, but there was always the few who believed only what they saw. Tall men were the more likely to become sniper victims. Most front-line trenches were dug and prepared to accommodate the average height soldier. For men over six feet, it must have been both difficult and painful to operate. I heard of one German soldier who walked into a British front trench at dawn one morning and gave himself up. His sole reason for doing so, so he said, was because of his height. He was six feet, four inches, and despite the fact that he had to carry out all of his assignments in a stooped-over agonizing position, the English soldiers were constantly taking pot-shots at him.

Even when we were as far as a mile or more behind our own front-line trench, we dared not raise our heads above the surface of the ground during the daylight hours. The Turks were experts in every kind of concealment and camouflage and somehow always managed to hide themselves in the most inconspicuous places. Wherever there was a slight depression in the ground, a small mound, or a scrub bush perhaps not more than two feet high, chances were two to one that a sharpshooter would be in or behind it, and if he once got his rifle sights in line with one's head, there was seldom if ever [a] need for a second shot, as every one of them appeared to be what our boys called crack shots. I do, however, have knowledge of one who missed, but only by a fraction of an inch. It was an amusing topic of conversation for a long time after ...

About a week or so after our arrival, five other boys and I were detailed from front-line duty and sent down to the landing beach to fetch back six two-gallon jars of rum that had been unloaded from the scows[1] earlier that morning. The rum would be issued to our regiment the following day. As I did not drink rum myself, nor did I like the smell of the stuff, I felt none too happy at being chosen as a pack mule for that particular kind of transportation. But later, when I realized how helpful it was in boosting the spirits and morale of so many of the boys suffering from trench feet, dysentery, yellow jaundice, and many other diseases common to Gallipoli, I underwent a complete change of heart. But despite the fact that I frequently felt just as trench weary, homesick, and despondent as any of the other boys, my stomach always rebelled every time that I tried to take a little of the rum myself.

The landing beach where all of our food, guns, and munitions were being unloaded from scows and barges was a very short distance from enemy front lines. It was constantly under shellfire both night and day. The probability of being killed or wounded there was at least twice as likely as it would have been in our own front-line trench. In fact, prior to the late-November torrential rains flooding and totally destroying our trenches and dugouts, our most advanced front-line firing trench was considered by everyone to be the least dangerous location on our side of the Gallipoli Peninsula.

On our way back from the beach, each of us carrying on our shoulder two jars of rum enclosed in a wood slat crate, we came to one of several low spots in the communication trench where, in order to prevent some sharpshooter who could be lurking nearby from using our heads as targets, it became necessary to move forward cautiously with our heads and shoulders in a downward stoop and as low as possible.

Walking one behind the other in single file, five of us made it in safely, but the boy in the rear (as he later admitted), in order to ease the ache in his back, straightened himself up a little just as he entered the low spot and — *Bang!* Fortunately, he was carrying the crate of rum on his left shoulder, which helped to hide and shield his head from the sniper's bullet. It took only seconds for the rest of us to hurry back to where he had fallen, but as he lay there in the bottom of the trench, saturated with rum and much more still dripping all over him, it was not possible to tell at first glance as to whether he was alive or dead. We raised him up to a sitting position so that we could examine the back of his head and neck, and almost immediately, he opened his eyes, sniffed a couple of times, took a long deep breath, and muttered, "Oh, what a pleasant and glorious way to die."

Except for a few light scratches and his torn trousers caused by the fall, he never had a cut or a mark on him, which made it that much more difficult to convince the boys up in the front-line trench that the whole affair had not been staged so that we could help ourselves to the extra rum. To make matters a whole lot worse, three of the boys, including the one shot at, having drunk the remainder of the rum still left in the neck of the jug after it broke, were as drunk as lords by the time we had made it all the way back to battalion headquarters.

Our platoon sergeant was even more suspicious, and knowing that I did not drink rum, came to me for details as to what really did happen. At first, I thought he must be joking and told him as much, stating that in my opinion nobody could possibly like rum well enough to risk being court-martialled for just a few drinks of the stuff. "Oh, no," he replied. "You don't know that big son of a bitch as well as I do. His family were neighbours of ours back home, and neither he nor his old man would let such a petty thing as a court martial stop them if there was a drink to be had. They are both typical booze hounds and will drink anything and everything that has a kick." Later, when I got to know the boy in question better, I was inclined to agree with the sergeant, as he sure was fond of his liquor. Nevertheless, he was one of the most fearless and enduring soldiers of the First World War, and less than a year later back in France, he proved it.

———

Disease was rampant — enteric and typhoid being the number-one killers. Many of our boys would be suffering from enteric fever, typhus, dysentery, and yellow jaundice all at the same time — some of them with so little control over their bowels that a mixture of blood and mucus could often be seen oozing from the bottoms of their trouser legs. If all the boys who should have been in hospital had been permitted to go, the Turks could have come over and killed, captured, or driven into the sea all that was left of us in just one afternoon.

During the daytime, the flies were so numerous that unless one put a blanket or a ground sheet over one's head, it was impossible to put a piece of bread or any kind of food in one's mouth without having a dozen or more flies going in with it. Then, at night, the ever-hungry tormenting lice took over, making life more miserable than I ever thought possible. If there was a hell during the First World War, it was the Dardanelles. If there were two, the other was Passchendaele, and I have already served time in both.

———

These conditions continued until the coming of winter. A furious storm destroyed the RNR trenches and a flash freeze took a terrible toll. The BEF evacuation of Gallipoli came soon after. Withdrawing an entire army from the exposed peninsula without the Turks pursuing was a risky endeavour — Manuel describes some of the methods used to succeed.

———

On the Suvla Bay side of the peninsula, where our battalion served for the first three months, every precious drop of water had to be shipped in by boat, which meant that some of us, except those brave souls who risked being killed or wounded by swimming in the Aegean Sea near the constantly shelled beach, never got to take a bath. In fact, we seldom if ever got enough water to quench our ever-burning thirst, especially on the days when the bay became too windy and rough for the boats to dock.

All through the summer months there had seldom been a drop of rain. Then suddenly, on a day in late November, the skies blackened and the heavens turned upside down. I had seen many rains and hurricane-force windstorms back home, but nothing I could compare to this one. Within minutes every last one of our trenches and dugouts, which consisted mostly of sand and sandbags, began to crumble, cave in, and wash away. We had worked our heads off for weeks, constructing sheet metal shelters, which we reinforced with several layers of sand bags placed over the top, meant to give us some protection against both the cold, stormy weather and enemy shell fragments, throughout the coming winter months. In less than twenty minutes every last one of them had filled back in with the water-soaked, flowing sand, and all of the sheet metal roofing and other building material had completely disappeared. Rifles not in use, equipment, and even heavy boxes of small arms ammunition were carried down the sloping terrain by the tremendous force of water, similar to logs being driven down a fast-flowing river.

Men of other regiments, located on very low land known as Salt Lake (but dry in summer), fared even worse than we did. The water having once reached the low spots kept rising so fast that some of them drowned before they could make it to higher ground. Many others barely escaped with their lives as they waded their way up through the quick-flowing sand.

That same evening, after everything had been totally destroyed, the winds shifted to the north, the rains turned to sleet, and before morning broke the sleet had turned to snow. It became bitterly cold and a horse and cutter could have driven over the ice that had formed overnight. Only those of us with the will and endurance to keep stomping our feet and exercising our bodies all through that long, bitter, cold night, managed to escape frostbite. A considerable number belonging to the 9th Brigade, holding the line on our right, having lost all their trenches and shelters and with no protection left them, other than the very lightweight summer uniforms that they were wearing when the storm broke, either froze to death or died from exposure during that never-to-be-forgotten, tragic night. When morning came, disorder and confusion lay everywhere.

During the days that followed, many thousands were invalided back to Mudros,[2] Alexandria, Malta, and several other Mediterranean base hospitals, as fast as ships could be provided to take them away, thereby hastening one of the most tragic and dismal failures of the First World War — our defeat and evacuation of the Dardanelles.

---

During the day, we moved about the trenches, firing an occasional rifle shot from here and there, laying booby traps with tripwires, and setting devices, which were meant to continue misleading the Turks until after the last of the rearguard garrison had departed. Some were kept busy preparing unmanned rifles to continue firing for hours, or even longer, after the trenches had been evacuated.

There were several methods for doing this. One was to suspend, from the trigger of a rifle that had been wired into position, a tin can partially filled with sand. Above it was another can filled with water, which very slowly leaked into the can below. When the combined weight of the sand

and water in the lower can amounted to about seven pounds, the trigger would be pulled and the rifle discharged. A second device employed a fuse attached to the wick of a lighted candle, which was sheltered by a biscuit tin, to detonate a Mills bomb[3] after a set period of time.

Picture, if you can, several thousand English and ANZAC [Australian and New Zealand Army Corps] troops crouched in a shallow, half-dug trench (or section of a trench) that they had wrested from their Turkish opponents the previous day, after a fierce struggle resulting in the loss of several hundred of their friends and countrymen.

Now picture orders coming through from one of our faraway, off-shore, safety-zone generals (none of whom has ever been seen by those very same men) that the trench must be held "at all cost." All of our ammunition has been used up, but apparently the Turks still have plenty, including shrapnel, bombs, and high-explosive shells. In addition to sweeping every foot of the terrain lying immediately behind the trench with rifle and machine-gun fire to keep our boys pinned down within the shallow trench, the Turks would unleash an overwhelming artillery fire barrage consisting of shrapnel and high-explosive shells, over and on the trench itself. [They] know that we are out of ammunition and cannot advance or attack without it, so they set about to exterminate as many of us as possible before nightfall.

When the welcomed and longed-for darkness arrived, at last, to hide them from the snipers and machine-gunners, less than 40 percent were fortunate enough to make the quarter mile back to their original front-line trench, from where they had started out before dawn the previous morning. That, owing to the lack of munitions, was as far as they ever got again. All of the other 60 percent including the seriously wounded (except the very few lucky ones who made it on the back of a comrade), were either killed or captured.

In the meantime, the shells they should have had, which would have undoubtedly made the difference between success and failure, to say nothing of the thousands of young lives that would have been spared, were being held back from the men on the Gallipoli Peninsula so that they could be properly counted, checked, and calculated. Maybe that was why we were getting less than 20 percent of the number of ammunitions being sent to France — it cost too much to ship them so far.

Sometime during the second week in December (I think it was the twelfth), we were told that both ANZAC[4] and Suvla[5] were to be evacuated, but Helles was to be retained, at least for the present and perhaps permanently. Apparently, those scheming, self-seeking politicians back at the War Office and the House of Commons in London were still manoeuvring and plotting for their own advancement, regardless of the fact that thousands of lives were depending on a final decision. I have read that there were a number of both officers and men at the ANZAC front who would much rather have stayed there for at least another week or so, which would have given them time to finish and blow up a network of mines that they had placed under the enemy's front trench. After months of tunnelling underground passageways across no man's land, it was said that many of the ANZACs (both Australians and New Zealanders) were bitterly disappointed at being compelled to abandon those elaborate defences that they had so skillfully designed and constructed in order to survive the winter weather plus the expected onslaught of enemy artillery.

On the nights of the 18th and 19th of December 1915, the last twenty thousand men of the ANZAC garrison, in superbly ordered progression, at three miles an hour, with either socks or sandbags over their boots and torn blankets over the floor of the trenches, folded their tents and stole away. The last parties moved back from their posts, in some places within ten yards of the enemy. "At twenty minutes to three, in the early morning of the twentieth, the ANZAC position on Lone pine" (wrote the official historian) "became open to the enemy."

Our evacuation of Suvla was little or no different from the one at ANZAC. On Sunday, December the nineteenth, those of us who were still left at Suvla did everything possible, or at least everything we knew how, to deceive the Turks. We moved from one traverse of the front-line trench to the next, firing a rifle shot or two from each traverse, or about the same number of shots that would have been fired had the trench held its full quota of men instead of less than 10 percent of them. This 10 percent rearguard had the responsibility of keeping the Turks in the dark until the very last moment of our departure, or until the 90 percent who were on their way to the beach and boats had arrived there. Should the Turks become aware of what we were up to and decide to attack, it was the duty of the rearguard to hold them back for as long as possible and to the last man if necessary. Whether it would have turned out that way if the Turks had attacked, who knows?

During our last two nights at Suvla, the well-planned schedule for the evacuation proceeded with clockwork precision. By midnight, we had all boarded the boats waiting to take us away. The impossible had been achieved. Close to ninety thousand men had been evacuated from Suvla and ANZAC, as well as 168 guns, a considerable number of animals, ammunition, stores, etc., and all without the loss of a single man.

But, unfortunately, as one writer put it, "Whatever hopes the boys in our regiment, the Newfoundlanders, may have entertained of a pro-longed, well-deserved rest on Imbros were soon shattered."[6] For about thirty hours, we enjoyed the unaccustomed comfort of hot food and shelter under canvas, and most of all the blessed freedom from the strain of front-line trench duty. Then suddenly, at midday on December twenty-second, came orders to re-embark. By three or four o'clock in the afternoon, all that was left of our regiment had boarded a small ship at Imbros harbour, where we were joined by other units of the 29th Division, all of whom, like ourselves, had only just got through the nerve-wracking [*sic*] evacuation of Suvla. We were now on our way (although we did not know it then) to do it all over again at Cape Helles, which, according to Lord Kitchener and most of our off-shore, safety-zone generals, was not to be evacuated after all. Instead, it was to be strengthened with six or more divisions from Salonika, plus several batteries of heavy guns from Suvla, ANZAC, and Britain.

———

An hour or so after our little ship had weighed anchor, she came to a full stop and lighters began taking us ashore at "W" Beach, also known as Lancashire Landing (named for the magnificent achievement of the 1st Lancashire Fusiliers in fighting their way ashore there nine months before). What a cruel and discouraging letdown. Instead of being on our way to Egypt, as we had been assured we would be following the evacu-ation of Suvla, we were again back in the trenches. What was left of the boys in our battalion (less than three hundred) were not just disappointed, they were outraged. Never before, nor since, have I ever heard so much complaining, cursing, and name-calling, much of which was of a kind that I had never heard before.

In fact, some of the boys were [as] close to open rebellion and mutiny as any group or company of men could be without actually taking an active part in one, and they had ample reason to be. After enduring three long frightening months, cooped up in stinking, slimy, grave-shaped trenches and often with hordes of bloated, corpse-eating rats and ugly poisonous scorpions, we were permitted to remain in Imbros just long enough to enjoy our first and only two hot, appetizing meals in over three long, heartbreaking months, before our luxury-living, off-shore strategists ordered us to some other part of the God-forsaken Gallipoli Peninsula to risk our necks all over again.

From the landing beach, our battalion went into divisional reserve. We found shelter in some old abandoned trenches, which we cleaned up and made as livable as possible. For a week or more, we repaired roads, dug trenches, and even constructed new ones. The Turks, however, from the higher ground, had a clear view of just about everything we did and were not being fooled. Even though our own scheming and plotting politicians back in London could not agree as to whether we should stay or leave, the German general Liman von Sanders (overall commander of the Turkish army and the most brilliant strategist on the Gallipoli Peninsula)[7] and Colonel Kannengiesser (his second-in-command) knew that sooner or later, we would leave rather than wait to be driven out, and as the good weather was not expected to hold much longer, it would have to be sooner, not later.

By January 7, 1916, the London War Office had finally come to a decision about Helles, and secret orders came through for its immediate evacuation. The French were the first to go, and units of what was left of the 29th Division were sent in to fill the gap and assist in directing the four divisions (about forty thousand men), still left in the bridgehead, to the beaches and boats. We were in a very tight spot, for even if we had hood-winked the enemy during the evacuation of Suvla and ANZAC (which I, for one, have never believed — and there were well over one hundred thousand other Gallipoli front-line veterans of the same opinion), it would not be possible to fool them a second time.

Although there existed a sense of hope that we would eventually be evacuated (provided the Turks with their extra thousands of troops from the Suvla and ANZAC fronts did not attack and kill us all in the meantime), there was no assurance that we would be. In fact, our company officers had, just the week before, received "orders of the day" cards, which definitely stated that Helles was not to be evacuated. For those who believed it — and there were many — the fear of being captured and becoming prisoners of war was even worse and more frightening than the fear of being killed, for there was a very strong rumour going the rounds that the Turks had castrated all of their recently captured prisoners and threatened to do the same to all those taken in future.

The plan for the evacuation of Helles followed the same pattern as the one used to evacuate Suvla and ANZAC. The four divisions holding the front-line trenches, four miles from the landing beaches, were gradually thinned out each night until only a rearguard force of less than one division, maybe eight or ten thousand men, remained. We Newfoundlanders were still in reserve but were ready to reinforce other battalions of the 88th Brigade, should the Turks attack. During the last two nights of the evacuation, traffic cards were issued to the various units, pointing out the routes they were to follow to the coast and where they were to be at stated intervals. Very little could be done for the large number of wounded, except to take them back to the wide-open beaches, where they lay under shellfire in the burning heat of the sun, parched with thirst. One of the war historians wrote, "It was left to the dead themselves to solve the problem of over-crowding."[8] Each morning, a trawler would make a trip to the three-mile limit, where their journey ended in a brief burial service.

Many years later, I read how on October 17, 1915, General Sir Ian Hamilton had sailed out of Gallipoli's Imbros Harbour for the last time. All of the sailors saluted and waved him farewell. I have also read that, regardless as to whether he was a first- or second-rate strategist, General Sir Ian Hamilton was one of the most respected and best-loved officers in the entire British army. Even the French officers, both army and navy (none of whom ever had any faith or confidence in high-ranking British officers of the First World War), came from their warships and battle-fronts to see him off and to express their regrets at his leaving. It was said that some of his staff actually shed tears as they watched his ship disappear beyond the horizon. It was as John North, author of *Gallipoli: The Fading Vision*, described him: "It is perhaps the finest compliment to Sir

Ian Hamilton's command, that with his departure, the last shred of spirit vanished from the campaign." North also wrote that if Gallipoli can ever be said to have a soul, it died that autumn afternoon.

The following is Sir Ian's farewell message to his Gallipoli soldiers: "You will hardly fade away until the sun fades out of the sky and the earth sinks into the universal blackness. For already you form part of that great tradition of the Dardanelles which began with Hector and Achilles. In another few thousand years the two stories will have blended into one and whether, when 'the iron roaring went up to the vaults of heaven through the unharvested sky,' as Homer tells us, it was the spear of Achilles, or whether it was a 100 lb shell from Asiatic Annie, won't make much odds to the Almighty ..."[9]

Much as I admire General [Hamilton] my Dardanelles experience had nothing to do [with] Hector, Achilles, or glorious war. We survived. The only pleasant memory I have of the Dardanelles, or of any other part of the Gallipoli Peninsula, is of a day in early January 1916 when I stood at the stern railing of the ship that was taking me back to Egypt and watched as it slowly faded from view in the distant horizon.

———

Manuel's Gallipoli story is a remarkable amalgam describing horrid living conditions, the Turkish enemy's proficiency, and eight months of emotionally draining risk of death on the exposed RNR beachhead position. His Gallipoli account is profoundly ironic. The relief Manuel remembers on seeing the Dardanelles Strait disappear over the horizon in January 1916 is soon supplanted by his experience of ceaseless death and human destruction, to which Beaumont-Hamel provides the grim climax.

# CHAPTER FOUR

## BEAUMONT-HAMEL, JULY 1916

"The Battle of the Somme" remains one of the most evocative expressions in Great War history. It symbolizes many of the popular conceptions of how the war was conducted — massive Allied assaults launched against well-fortified, determined German defenders. The first Allied Somme offensive was intended to relieve German pressure on Verdun, the strategically important French city to the south. An intense, sustained, ten-day artillery barrage followed by a concerted ground offensive striking at German positions along a twenty-mile front was the core British strategy. Over twenty thousand Allied dead and sixty thousand casualties on July 1, 1916, is a grim testament to its failure.

Not surprisingly, how Manuel remembers the Somme and Beaumont-Hamel over sixty-five years after these battles is far from a dispassionate historical account. His reminiscence is coloured by a blend of disgust for the British leadership that ordered the RNR forward that bright morning of July 1, and undiminished sadness for the loss of his Newfoundland comrades. Valour, glory, and noble death for a righteous cause were the contemporary descriptions frequently conveyed in the Allied nations' media accounts of the Somme. Manuel offers anger, disgust, and sorrow that are undiminished by time. It is in his Beaumont-Hamel accounts that Manuel intersperses conventional Great War criticisms of Allied leadership, particularly the command of Sir Douglas Haig, with a searingly personal recollection of what happened to him and his regiment when they went "over the top" at 8:05 a.m.

———

After our defeat in the Dardanelles, our regiment, or what was left of it, was transported back to Egypt, where, for the following two months at Port Suez, near the Red Sea, we kept licking our wounds while regaining our strength and preparing for the Western Front. Early in the spring of 1916, after a boat trip up the Mediterranean and a train trip across France, we reached the Somme battlefront.

A few weeks prior to embarking for Egypt and the Dardanelles in 1915, seven other boys and I, considered to be fairly good hunters and marksmen, were chosen for a special scout-training course. It was a very interesting assignment and the only job I ever had in the army that I really liked. On the whole, I hated army life and everything connected or pertaining to it; both in the trenches and out. I could never understand why any young man would want to become a soldier in peacetime or choose it as a permanent occupation, unless of course he had the ambition plus the qualifications to become a professional brass hat. Personally, if given no other alternative, I would much prefer to dig ditches for a livelihood.

In most previous wars, scouting had been a most necessary and vital assignment, but there was very little work for a scout to perform in trench warfare. There was no need for long marches or hikes through the forest or desert in order to track down and gather information regarding the enemy's whereabouts, strength, and the like. We always knew exactly where he was and often wished we didn't. How to get him out of there was something nobody seemed to know, least of all the generals.

On leaving the Dardanelles, the few of us left became sharpshooters. We were still members of what was known as the Intelligence Department, but that fancy name was retained only to disguise the nasty label of "*sniper.*" If one could shoot straight, it required no more "intelligence" to be a sniper than it did to be a trench digger, a mule driver, or any of the other front-line assignments. We were issued high-powered telescopic rifles, field glasses, and a pass permit that would allow us to use any part of the terrain that we considered best for the purpose. One of our members so fittingly described it at the time, "We have now been presented with a wholesale licence to go out and commit murder." That was precisely the way I felt about it. I'll never forget his words. Except in case of attack or emergency, we were freed from all other duties and could rest the whole night through. It was undoubtedly the easiest and laziest kind of work of all front-line assignments and many of our comrades, who so often had to stand guard night and day, were envious of what they called our cushy jobs. Despite the extra ease and comfort, I was just not the type for that kind of fighting. I detested everything about it, so much so that I soon made up my mind to apply for a transfer to some other kind of work, even at the risk of being thought of as a weakling, or perhaps something much worse.

No special courage is required to shoot at someone who is already shooting at you and your friends, or who is coming at you with a bayonet. It is either his life or yours, and if you are fortunate enough to get him before he gets you that is self-preservation. While you might feel sorry for what you were compelled to do, you don't feel as sick and dirty inside for weeks or months or perhaps for all time afterward as you do in the job of a sniper. Having the head of some poor unsuspecting man or boy lined up in the sights of a powerful telescopic rifle, and being dead certain that as soon as your finger squeezes the trigger that man or boy will never breathe or even be given another chance of seeing his loved ones again, is something altogether different. Not only could it cause a sensitive, conscientious person to feel sick and dirty for days and weeks, it could haunt and torment him for as long as he lived.

Had it been possible to shoot those German men and boys in the arms or legs or some part of the body where they would have had a fighting chance of survival, I would have done so willingly and eagerly. I very much doubt if there were one single front-line soldier on either side of no man's land who would not have welcomed any honourable way out of that horrible godforsaken death trap. But, unless they were out of their trenches in open terrain, few snipers seldom got to see more than their heads; most often just the bare tops of their helmets.

One is apt to know and become good friends with many other boys in his regiment, but there is seldom more than one who appeals to him as a kindred spirit; one in whom he could confide his innermost thoughts, doubts, and fears, feeling sure within himself that, whatever the subject confided or discussed, no part of it will ever be divulged to a third party. I was very fortunate in having just such a friend. He was a sergeant in the Signal Corps and one of the finest young men that ever went to sea. His father owned a couple of fishing schooners and he had skippered one of them prior to joining the regiment the previous year. He felt much the same way about sniping as I did and agreed that no one should have to do it against his will, or if it caused him to feel guilty or distressed. Not only did he understand and sympathize as to how I felt, he suggested a solution whereby I could obtain a transfer without any of my friends knowing that I had requested one. I had some doubts as to whether I could qualify for the kind of work he had in mind, but I was willing and quite eager to try.

The sergeant suggested that I carry on with the work I was assigned to for the time being, but spend as much time as possible learning how to operate the various kinds of signal equipment, such as heliograph, telegraph, and phillorphone sets. Fortunately, I already knew the Morse code. It had been part of our scout-training course during our stay in Egypt, but I needed practice and much of it in order to qualify as a front-line signaller. The sergeant loaned me a book of signals and a small telegraph buzzer to practise on, promising to help me as much as possible whenever he could find the time to do so. He was quite sure that as soon as I had acquired sufficient practice there would be no difficulty whatever in arranging a transfer, because communication had priority over all other assignments and signallers were not being trained fast enough. There weren't sufficient numbers at our base headquarters in Scotland to fill the gaps caused by the high rate of casualties suffered by front-line signallers.

Among the various hideouts and observation posts that I made use of as a sniper (I still hate to write the nasty name) was one that I had constructed and camouflaged myself. It was similar to some of those used by the Turks in the Dardanelles, and because it was a rather difficult post to enter and leave without being seen from one particular sector of the German front trench, nobody ever bothered to visit me. So in that hideout for the following eight weeks, in between rest periods, instead of scanning the German front-line trenches and the surrounding terrain, as I was supposed to have done, I spent every moment tapping the key of that little telegraph buzzer, stopping just long enough now and then to rest my aching fingers. My friend was pleased with the progress I had made in such a short time, so a couple of weeks later, during another behind-the-line rest period, and without any questions being asked, I was told to turn in all of my sniper's equipment and report to the signal officer.

A couple of months later, on July 1st, we arrived opposite a village named Beaumont-Hamel, which was occupied by the Germans. We took part in one of the bloodiest, one-sided massacres, plus the biggest defeat in all of British history, on a front about fifteen miles wide. In less than three hours, the British army suffered sixty thousand casualties (twenty thousand of which were fatal) — the most casualties in any army in any one day in all time. To the best of my knowledge, not one man in our whole division got as far as the enemy's front lines, located just four or five hundred yards from our own.

In less than ten minutes after leaving our foxholes and trenches, every gap cut in our own barbed wire entanglements the previous night to provide us with a passageway through for the attack in the morning, was filled with dead and dying men. I was out in no man's land not more than twenty-five minutes (probably less) and had got to within thirty or so yards of the enemy's barbed wire before getting the main artery in my right forearm severed with machine-gun bullets. By then, I had lost two rifles and was carrying a third — the first and second having been shattered and rendered useless by the overwhelming enemy fire. Although the mortars, shrapnel, and shellfire was beyond anything that I had ever witnessed either before or after, well over 90 percent of our casualties resulted from machine-gun fire — the weapon that our Commander-in-Chief, Sir Douglas Haig, when asked by the Minister of Munitions how many he needed, replied, "The machine gun is a much overrated weapon and two for each battalion will be more than sufficient."

The thousands of seriously wounded, unable to make it back in on their own, had found temporary protection from rifle and machine guns (but not shells) in the deeper shell craters. Talking with some of those boys (both the rescued and the lads who had helped to rescue them) back in a London hospital a week or so later, they told me something about that terrifying first night and the nerve-wracking nights that followed. The Germans, being well aware that every effort would be made to bring in from no man's land as many of the wounded as could be found, kept up a murderous bombardment all through the night. In addition to every kind of artillery fire, they continued to rake and sweep every yard of no man's land with rifle and machine-gun bullets, thereby killing or wounding perhaps a third as many as were rescued.

Before dawn broke on that second dreadful morning, over 80 percent of the stretcher-bearers had been either killed or wounded, but despite the frightful danger to themselves, those boys went voluntarily out into that awesome exploding inferno, night after night, until they felt reasonably sure that no other men were left out there alive. Unfortunately, some men were indeed left out there who were still alive. It would have been utterly impossible to search all of the millions of shell holes during the darkness of night. One of our wounded Newfoundland boys who had arrived in France and joined the battalion only the night before the attack crawled back into our own front-line trench one morning after spending five days and nights in a shell hole near the German wire, trying to decide which trench was which; fortunately he guessed the right one ... or maybe not. Sadly, he was killed later in the war.

They mentioned one lad in particular who insisted on going out night after night to look for his younger brother, but every time he saw a wounded man, he would postpone the search for his brother to bring the wounded man in. On his last trip out, he never returned. They found him between two shell holes the following night, and the man he had been carrying on his back when he was killed was still not his brother. Greater love hath no man.

———

Manuel is deeply critical of the English military leadership through-out his memoir. The Somme accounts illustrate this theme particularly well. Much of the chapter is scattered with his passionate criticism of British officer ineptitude. Shortly after the RNR was virtually wiped out at Beaumont-Hamel, the regiment was ordered back into action. Manuel provides this particularly scathing description.

———

When our colonel, who did not go over the top with us, was informed of the total destruction of his regiment, he reported the information back to his superiors. They were shocked, or so they said, at the appalling number of casualties suffered, but what followed an hour or so later proved that they were far more concerned and disappointed because of our failure to take our objectives rather than sorry or saddened by the frightful number of dead and wounded. Within a few minutes of the colonel's report, one of those faraway, incompetent, irresponsible brass hats phoned battalion headquarters and informed the colonel that regardless of the cost in casualties, the Germans must be driven from their trenches and beaten back and the colonel was to immediately round up every available man who was still capable of holding a rifle and renew the attack on the enemy's front line.

The colonel, of course, like everyone else in Sir Douglas Haig's army, dared not talk back or question the orders of his superior — even though he was well aware that such an order could only be coming from one of the remote-base-located, safety-zone, luxury-living brass hats who had never once, during the more than four years of war, ventured close enough to a fighting front to get just one small speck of mud on their luxurious, Beau Brummell, fifty-guinea riding boots.

In *The Somme*, written by General Sir Anthony Heritage Farrar-Hockley,[1] [the author] explains why our regiment suffered such an appalling loss on that dreadful 1st of July day. Here, in part, is what he writes:

> The two leading battalions of the 88th Brigade, 29th Division — the Newfoundland and Essex Regiments — were to move forward individually. One, the Essex, could not reach no man's land. They were physically obstructed by the endless lines of wounded in every trench and deep shell holes…. German gunners had shelled this section of the British fire support and reserve trenches extensively at 7:35 with terrible success. The Newfoundlanders were ordered to continue alone. They had already advanced in the open to take cover in the forward shell holes from where they would wait for their zero hour. At 9:05 they rose and marched forward in open ranks, half turned toward Y Ravine, newcomers to the zone of destruction. Almost in unison, the machine guns fired from Y Ravine … if the line of men perseveres

with a determined gallantry over a long open approach, the end is certain. So it was before Y Ravine. The officers and men of the Newfoundland Regiment would not halt; they had been ordered to advance into the enemy line. They advanced; they fell.[2]

I have no intention of questioning any part of his generous compliment to the men of our regiment except to say that if it was gallantry in my own particular case that kept me going, then gallantry and deadly fear must be one and the same thing, or at least have a great deal in common with each other. For it was fear, not fearlessness, but stark-naked fear that accompanied me every step of the way across the flaming inferno of no man's land. The fear of letting my friends and comrades down by chickening out and taking cover in one of the many inviting shell holes seemed to be that much more terrifying than the fear that kept urging and forcing me forward. I kept wondering if any or many of the other boys felt as I did and continued to push themselves in the direction of the blazing guns for the same reason.

Regardless as to whether it was fear or gallantry (or perhaps some of both) that kept every last man in our regiment on his feet and heading east until dead or helpless men [who] could go no farther, it never should have happened and was, in my opinion, one of the biggest mistakes that any body of men has ever made. Regardless of what the orders were or from whence they came, we should have ignored them and taken cover in some of the nearby shell holes immediately when those deadly machine-gun bullets began dropping our comrades beside us, particularly so when we already knew for sure that further effort on our part to reach and penetrate the German front trench was not only useless, but hopeless, and could serve only to get us all killed or wounded, which, of course, it did.

As maybe I mentioned before, if courage alone could have won on that beautiful, but tragic, July morning, we would have been well on our way to the Rhine River by evening. Never before had there ever been a more spirited and enthusiastic body of very young men — particularly so the many thousands of young wartime volunteer members of what was then known as Kitchener's New Army, most of whom would be going over the top for the first time that morning, and, unfortunately, for half or more of them, it would be the last (as with the boys in my own regiment who would be going along with them). Their courage and morale was at its peak, but, unfortunately, courage and morale alone was no protection against the numerous nests of death-spitting machine guns, any one of which was quite capable of destroying a whole battalion of men even before they had covered the first hundred yards across no man's land.

According to the "grapevine news," as it was called (about the only kind we ever heard up in the front-line trenches), some of our autocratic safety-zone generals were so confident that a great British victory was about to be won, they didn't even wait for the attack to begin before inviting their English friends and bluebloods over to their luxurious chateau headquarters to join them in the great victory celebration. I recall one of our battalion officers reading us a kind of pep or "cheerio" message from one of those safety-zone bigwigs in which (after several paragraphs of meaningless flattery and patriotic flag-waving) he wrote: "If everything proceeds as planned and I am confident it will, tomorrow's great victory will either be the end, or the beginning of the end, of the war; in either case, we shall all be back home to spend Christmas with our families and friends. What a victory, what a Christmas."

Well, over 60 percent of all those who heard the officer read that spiel were either dead or disabled within the next twenty-four hours, and for the few of us fortunate to have survived, home, family, and friends seemed farther away than ever.

During the Battle of the Somme on July 1st, 1916, not one single soldier in our whole brigade got farther than the near side of the enemy's barbed wire, and the few brave but unfortunate souls who managed to make it that far never lived to come back. Most of them were either bombed or machine-gunned to death while so desperately trying to cut their way through to the German front trench.

It was definitely not the lack of courage that prevented our boys from winning on that beautiful midsummer day. Although many of us were frightened, sore, and afraid for our lives, everyone kept heading in the same direction until dead and badly wounded men could go no further — none of us were shot in the back who had not first been shot in the front. The wonder is not why we failed to reach the enemy's front-line trench, but rather, how any of us ever survived long enough to make it back to our own.

Fortunately, the fifty-three men in our regiment who had escaped being wounded (or wounded seriously enough to be hospitalized) were all out at the first-aid station, helping the stretcher-bearers and the Red Cross boys in taking care of the wounded who had been struck down by shellfire while waiting their turn in the trenches and foxholes to climb over the top into no man's land, but I doubt very much that the colonel would have found any of them to send back into the blazing inferno for a second time in one day, even if they had been close by and available.

Later that same afternoon, a seriously wounded colonel in charge of an English battalion that had suffered casualties almost equal to our own was determined that his few surviving men must not be sent back into that roaring inferno to die helplessly, hopelessly, and to no purpose, and although suffering much pain, he insisted on talking to some of the divisional and corps commanders over one of the company's telephones — and having fought and fallen with his men, no battalion commander in all France was better qualified to give an eyewitness account of the whole horrible tragic situation. He was a soldier's soldier type of commander who insisted on going into battle with his men — the kind of leader who was admired and respected by every common front-line soldier in France. He was an officer whose men would have followed him to hell and back, if that were possible.

He told them of the frightful loss of life [and] of the many, many thousands of seriously wounded men and teenage boys who were still out there, hiding in shell holes and craters all over no man's land, waiting and praying for darkness and the hope of being rescued. Thousands of them were so badly wounded as to be absolutely helpless and suffering all the torments of hell from the heat and the flies and unable to quench their burning thirst from the water in their own bottles. He gave them a detailed description of the enemy's impregnable defence fortifications, plus their overwhelming firepower, from both artillery and machine guns, and finally managed to convince them of the utter futility in sending his few remaining men back out there to perish.

Picture sixty thousand men and boys — a number equal to an entire city population — all of them having been shot down in a narrow strip of shell-churned terrain less than fifteen miles in length and averaging about five to six hundred yards in depth (about as wide as a modern four-lane highway), all in just one morning. Twenty thousand of them are lying there dead between the two front trenches in no man's land, with perhaps half or more of the forty thousand wounded lying beside them (and in the shell holes nearby), too badly hurt to make it back into their own front trenches without assistance. The German front trench has not been breached. In fact, by this time, German resistance has been further strengthened by thousands of extra men and guns from their support trenches, making them that much better prepared to withstand and repulse any further attacks.

Despite all of the devastation and disaster, plus the frightful loss of life and in broad daylight, battalion and company commanders were being ordered, by remote control from their fifty-mile-beyond-the-danger-zone superiors, to assemble all of the men still capable of holding a rifle and send them back into that terrifying death trap, from where their chances of ever coming out alive would be less than a hundred to one.

I am well aware that the following will read as being incredible and beyond belief to anyone other than those who may have taken some part in it (and only a very few who did are alive at the time of this writing). Believe it or not, prior to going over the top on that never-to-be-forgotten 1st of July, 1916, morning, we were given strict and rigid orders of what (and what not) to do and told that if we disobeyed or disregarded any of them, we could be court-martialled and shot by a firing squad.

We were warned that, regardless of what happened on our way across no man's land, we must not, "under any circumstances," fall out or stop to take cover from enemy fire. We [were ordered to] continue to advance at a steady regulation pace, in open ranks and in precise military formation, until we reached and took possession of the enemy's front-line trench. [We would] kill or capture any of the surviving Germans [from] our week-long artillery bombardment on the enemy's front trench and barbed wire. Sir Douglas and his top generals who assisted him in planning the Somme offensive were confident that the bombardment [had] totally destroyed the [entire German] front-line defences and rendered [their] firing line untenable and useless.

As no resistance was to be expected until after we had paraded across no man's land in precise military formation and taken possession of the supposedly ruined and deserted German trenches, providing us with any kind of artillery support on our way over would not be necessary;

and that, according to the staff major, was why the German snipers and machine-gunners were left free and unmolested to gun us down at will — and gun us down they did. They dropped us in long, extended lines and rows like so many drifts of ripened grain that had been raked for harvest until, as an eyewitness German officer later wrote, "It appeared as though there was no longer enough space left in any part of no man's land for another British soldier to fall without falling on the body of one of his countrymen."[3]

Like so many others, I was hit and immediately jumped in one of the deepest nearby shell holes, with the intention of remaining there until nightfall, which was still more than twelve hours away, but the whiz-bangs[4] and other types of shells began to explode all around me, one of which came close enough to splash several inches of mud all over me, so after bandaging up my arm as best I could and getting rid of all equipment except for my water bottle, gas mask, and emergency ration, I decided (or rather, something seemed to tell me) that I should hurry and get the hell out of there.

I was more fortunate than most of the other boys. I could still walk, but I didn't walk — I ran — and ran as though the devil himself was chasing me. I did not panic, although I doubt if I was far from doing so. My hunting instinct warned me not to try making it all the way back across no man's land in just one lap, so I used the "stop and go" system — running from one shell hole to another, just a few yards farther on, as fast as my trembling legs could carry me. Although I did not know it then, this was the method used by both the French and Germans, except that they were using it to advance and attack the enemy, while I was doing so to run away from him.

As always, there were some who (although helpless and unable to move by themselves) insisted on waiting for aid until others who appeared to be in greater need had been taken care of. Many of the less seriously wounded who had been held down in the numerous shell holes by enemy fire all day made it back in on their own as soon as it became dark enough to hide them from the machine-gunners and snipers, and I was told that about one in every three who came in brought a more seriously wounded man in on his back. Some of the most tragic cases were those who had lain out in the blazing hot July sun all day, alone in a shallow shell hole, suffering intense pain and too seriously injured and helpless to reach for their own full water bottles to quench their burning daylong thirst. Many such cases died before they could be rescued — and others, shortly after.

This was the battle our divisional general had, on June 26 (just four days before), assured us would either end the war or be the beginning of the end. In either case, we would all be back home in time to spend Christmas with our families and friends. One hundred and ten thousand very young men (a third or more of them still in their teens), all volunteers, took part in that 1st day of July slaughter. One-fifth, twenty thousand of them, including my lifelong companion and most of my friends and comrades, were all dead before sunset that evening — most of them within minutes of leaving their foxholes and trenches. Another two-fifths, forty thousand, were wounded, many of whom suffered and died in agony while waiting for darkness and the hope of being rescued. The remaining two-fifths, the forty thousand survivors, would live to fight another day, but the odds were that most of them would either be killed or wounded, together with the half million others that were to follow between then and the freeze-up in November.

According to a wounded artillery officer at our London hospital, no arrangement had ever been made to have the barrage of artillery fire returned back on the enemy's firing line, in case we ran into strong rifle and machine-gun resistance on our way across no man's land. Because no such arrangements had been made, or emergencies provided for, the German machine-gunners and riflemen (all of whom, together with their guns and ammunition) had remained safe and comparatively comfortable in the bottoms of their forty-feet-deep, shell-proof dugouts during the entire seven days of continuous bombardment on their barbed wire and front-line trench.

Nobody knew why, or at least nobody has ever explained why ... instead of keeping the curtain of artillery fire on the enemy's front-line firing trench and barbed wire until we had covered the greater part of the way across no man's land and were within charging distance of their trench, it was redirected to random hit-or-miss targets, far beyond where it would have helped us.

———

Manuel's account of the RNR slaughter at Beaumont-Hamel does not break new military history ground. What Manuel reinforces in his account is the mindlessness and futility of the Somme assault tactics where the common soldier bears the brunt of failure. Manuel's physical pain, serious wounds, and long recovery are secondary to his contempt for the British leadership that he holds solely accountable for the RNR losses and the notion that his fellow Newfoundlanders sacrificed so much for so little.

# CHAPTER FIVE

## ENGLAND, AUTUMN 1916

Manuel was luckier than many of his RNR comrades in the Beaumont-Hamel aftermath. Taken to England (3rd London General Hospital, Wandsworth) for what was a year-long convalescence, Manuel describes his military hospital stay with considerable fondness. The war's realities intrude again for Manuel in early 1917. He is adamant that men completely unfit to fight were regularly pressured into re-enlistment, given grave British manpower shortages resulting from the war of attrition that became the dominant combat motif.

———

The king was always a very welcome visitor at Wandsworth, where two hundred or more boys from our regiment were being treated for wounds following the Somme front July 1st, 1916, massacre. The wish to have the king visit us as often as possible was not a very patriotic one, I suppose I should be ashamed to admit. It did not spring from the heart, but from the stomach. With each and every one of his visits, which were all too few, we were treated to a delicious roast beef dinner with at least twice the usual amount of meat. Moreover, it was served on nice bright china dishes, which seemed to make it much more palatable than if served on the old worn tin plates — the only kind we ever saw, except during the king's visits. He was barely out the door before the nurses and orderlies were rushing through the rooms and wards with their wagons and carts, gathering up the beautiful chinaware, which we would not see again until the king's next visit. We all hoped it would not be too long in coming.

There were certain simple rules that a sick or wounded soldier must abide by during the king's tour of inspection through the various wards. If the soldier was well enough to leave his bed, he must stand at attention beside it while the king was present. If he was asked any questions, he must address the king as "Sir, yes sir" and "No sir," which was not to be enlarged upon unless especially requested. The questions usually asked by the king were, "How are you?" and "Where were you wounded?" But the one most frequently asked and to a much greater number of patients was "Have you any complaints?" to which we were supposed to say, "No," regardless of the many we could have made. But who among us would be so ungrateful as to make complaints after just being served such a fine roast beef dinner?

Well, there was at least one soldier who apparently did not agree and had been waiting some time for just such an opportunity to unburden himself. He was one of the older soldiers — a Yorkshire man who, when the king asked if he had any complaints, snapped back, "Yes, I have complaints!"

"I am very sorry to hear that," the king said. "What are your complaints?"

Pointing his finger down the corridor, he said to the king, "You see that soldier in the fourth bed from the door? Well, he was shot in the testicles, but as you can see, I was shot in the throat, and every second morning, when the doctor for this ward comes on duty, he attends to that soldier's needs first, and after pawing around with the man's private parts for half an hour or longer and without washing his hands, he comes and pokes his fingers down my throat. Yes, I should bloody well think I have complaints." Needless to say, the king was embarrassed and his escort got him away from there pretty damn quick …

———

At various times during his convalescence in England, Manuel took the opportunity to travel to London to visit libraries and see the city. The English hospital authorities and their country house patrons provided limousine travel for the recovering soldiers to take advantage of a "day out." This account of a House of Commons debate Manuel saw in late 1916 is especially evocative.

———

After about three months at the Wandsworth Hospital, it was my good fortune to be sent to a little town named Esker on or near the Thames River and not far from London, where I spent several weeks in a great big beautiful mansion house that had been loaned or leased to the government and was operated by the Red Cross people as a convalescent home for sick and wounded veterans. It was a magnificent estate — the kind of place that only a member of the so-called filthy rich could afford to maintain. All the nurses except the matron in charge were rich or members of rich families who served without pay. Filthy rich or not, they were real ladies and all of their patients loved and admired them. This was something that could not be said of the disciplinarian old matron who was (or had been) a regular peacetime army nurse. Most of the young soldiers hated her guts and generally referred to her as "that miserable old bitch," mainly because she would not permit them to smoke inside or sit outside on the grass with their girlfriends.

Every day except Sundays, several luxurious, chauffeured limousine cars would come and take some of us in turn to London, to see a show, visit art galleries, museums, or just take us for a ride through the beautiful countryside. I had put my name in for a visit to the House of Commons. Eventually I was permitted to go.

We arrived and were shown to our seats a full half hour or longer before the House was called to order. The debate was mainly about the Dardanelles so, having served there the previous year, I was very much interested in hearing what the politicians had to say about it. After listening to several of the back benchers of both parties express their pro and con opinions, none of which was something we had not already read or heard about many times before, I soon lost interest. Then suddenly, the applause became deafening as Mr. David Lloyd George, who was secretary for war, prior to becoming prime minister, entered the Chamber and took the floor. From his very first sentence, I felt glued to my seat and apparently so was just about everyone else who heard him.

A quiet and meaningful stillness seemed to have descended on the entire House of Commons and, except for an occasional applause period, only his soft musical voice could be heard. I was thrilled as never before and only once or twice since. He did not spend too much time on the Dardanelles — just long enough to put the cause for its failure precisely where it belonged — on the Asquith government and its minister of war and supplies. He spoke of their failing to send half the number of troops required for a successful landing and followup during the first and second month of the campaign. He also mentioned their neglect to supply the few they did send with more than a third of the weapons and munitions needed to do the job. He had previously written that the footsteps of our soldiers on the Gallipoli Peninsula had been forever dogged by the mocking spectre of "too little" and "too late."

Lloyd George's friend, Mr. Churchill, was no longer a member of the cabinet. After our defeat in the Dardanelles, as first sea lord of the admiralty, he was falsely accused of being responsible for its failure. He was excluded from the newly formed Asquith war cabinet and permitted to leave for France to fight in the trenches. It is no wonder that we came within a hair's width of losing the war when such a brilliant mind as Winston Churchill was no longer considered an asset to the war effort and was allowed to leave for France to fight in the trenches and take orders from old, has-been generals. Such men knew less about how to fight, operate, and win a modern twentieth-century war than he had forgotten.

About six weeks after our visit, Mr. Lloyd George replaced Mr. Asquith as prime minister and one of his very first acts was to order his friend Churchill back from the trenches and appoint him as minister of munitions, where his energy and ability had been sorely needed....

After spending over four and a half months at Wandsworth, I was classified as being no longer fit for active front-line service. I was sent to our base headquarters up in Ayrshire, Scotland, for further treatment and convalescence. A considerable number of the boys there had recently been invalided back from the various Mediterranean hospitals — many of them still suffering from dysentery, jaundice, and several other diseases contracted in the Dardanelles. Many no longer fit for duty in France were awaiting their discharge and eagerly looking forward to the voyage back home, but unfortunately, quite a few of them never got to make it.

Shortly after breakfast one morning, we were informed by one of the medical staff that the CO had just received an important communiqué from the War Office. He wanted everyone who could walk over at the mess hall by one o'clock to hear what it was all about. It turned out to be what most of us had already suspected. Our battalion had again been in open battle and had suffered very heavy losses, and the need for reinforcements was desperately urgent. The CO said he fully realized that most of us had previously been classified as being no longer physically fit for front-line duty, but he thought perhaps there may be some among us who the medical officer would be willing to reclassify, if we cared to volunteer.

The CO was quite a student of human nature. He must have known that by wording his appeal in such a manner, it would take as much or more courage to say no than it would to say yes. As a result, every last man in the mess hall volunteered. Most of us, however, were confident of being rejected after a checkup — particularly so, those of us with wounds that were still causing some discomfort. Frankly, I rather doubt if any of the boys there were still so overwhelmed by patriotism as to prefer going back to all that misery and horrifying slaughter for a second (and for some of us, a third) time. If there were, I most definitely was not one of them. Never having been one of the heroic types, I could barely keep my legs from giving way under me on the eve of each and every battle that I ever took part in, and my stomach was forever full of fluttering butterflies.

I recall a lecture by one of the numerous generals stationed at Aldershot, where we received our final two weeks' training prior to embarking for Egypt and the Dardanelles: "Your first open hand-to-hand battle with the enemy," he said, "will be, by far, the worst on your nervous system. Each succeeding engagement will be much less frightening, and after just a very few battles, your sense of fear will completely disappear."

Well, I was in open battle several times, but for me, the general's theory always seemed to work in reverse. The more battles I took part in, the more frightened I became, and I could never forget that wise old adage about the pitcher that went to the well just once too often.

Either the general possessed an altogether different kind of physical structure from any of the men I knew, or, as I suspected then and have been sure of ever since, all of his open hand-to-hand battles had been fought with army textbooks at his very comfortable Aldershot headquarters. Any of the boys who confided in me readily admitted to being scared stiff on the eve of every open battle, regardless as to how many they had taken part in before. It is quite true, however, that some of us showed our fears more than others, but that was no sign of our being less courageous. I knew a boy in my platoon who, during the next-to-last attack that I ever took part in, trembled and shook to such an extent while waiting for the signal to go that I felt sure he was going to chicken out. I was never more wrong. Once over the top, I could not keep pace with him, and later, in another battle, he was awarded the military medal for daringly manoeuvring his way behind the enemy's trench and hurling a couple of Mills bombs through the back entrance of a machine-gun nest that had been keeping his company pinned down.

By the time the CO had finished with his patriotic flag-waving spiel for volunteers, the medical officer was all set up and ready to receive us. But instead of checking on our wounds and other physical disabilities, he just stood beside one of the mess tables. As we filed past, he asked each and every one of us the very same question phrased in a manner whereby a negative reply, unless one was on crutches or in a wheelchair, would be the equivalent of saying, "I am a coward and want to go home." It was only afterwards that some of the boys realized how readily they had fallen for this cunning little scheme, one that must have been concocted between the CO and medical officer prior to our mess hall arrival.

Half, or more, of the sick and wounded were as mad as hell on discovering how cunningly they had been tricked. They refused to leave for France until they had been given a thorough checkup by a qualified medical board, for which nobody blamed them because they were totally unfit for further active service. During the months that followed, between then and the Armistice (and particularly so during my POW starvation days in the slave labour camp), I was to regret and reproach myself a thousand times over for lacking the guts to have joined them. A week or so later, those of us who did not protest were back in France up to our knees — frequently as far as our bottoms, in the oozing Flanders blood-soaked mud.

Most of that spring and early summer, our regiment fought in the vicinity of Ypres and Passchendaele. I ended up at Steenbeck,[1] and anyone who ever fought there would, I am sure, agree that it was the most desolate

God-forsaken bogland in or around the whole entire Western Front. The quagmire was never less than six inches deep and frequently all the way up to our knees.

———

Manuel thus finds himself returning to France to fight at the Ypres Salient, where he would soon experience the horrors of the 1917 Passchendaele offensive.

# CHAPTER SIX

## PASSCHENDAELE, AUGUST 1917

For Manuel, Passchendaele is a depressing confirmation that the Allied leadership learned nothing from the Somme campaign. It remained business as usual along the front. Bombardment, trench raids, battles where yards of territory were won and lost with the numbing, deadly sameness. Passchendaele also marks the end of Manuel's combat experience. He will spend the next seventeen months as a German prisoner of war.

———

Passchendaele, like the Somme the year before — both of which were planned by the very same generals — was not actually a battle at all. In a real battle, both sides are more or less placed in a position to either shoot or bayonet each other, but in the so-called Third Battle of Ypres, only the German boys possessed that privilege. Therefore, it could not rightfully be described or classed as a battle, but the 310,000 British Empire youths who fell there knew well enough what it was. It was slaughter, absolute out and out slaughter, and because those German machine-gunners and riflemen had been provided with the strongest fortified defence system ever devised, either before or since, they were the boys who did well over 80 percent of the slaughtering.

Those ridiculous stories about the German soldiers being poor fighters that our newspapers insisted on printing for such a long time after the war began[1] probably originated with our luxury-living safety-zone generals, none of whom ever came close enough to a battlefield to see any soldiers in action — either German or British. Such stories most definitely did not originate with any front-line soldiers, either French or British, who unfortunately knew all too well the courage and endurance of their German opponents across the way and would have been only too happy if those phony press reports had contained some measure of truth.

I doubt very much if those Canadian boys who had been called in to spearhead a new attack, after the rest of us had been bogged down in the knee-deep mud and quagmire for eighty days, would consider any of those German lads they confronted in the rubble and ruins of Passchendaele Village as demoralized or on the verge of total collapse — a collapse that Sir Douglas had been assuring the Prime Minister and his Cabinet, ever since launching his foolhardy, foredoomed assault three months prior, could come at any moment. They could not have suffered eighteen thousand casualties in such a short time just shooting or bayonetting cowering Germans in the bottom of a trench, crying and begging for mercy, or standing with their hands high above their heads, pleading to be taken as prisoners of war. Nor could they have won those Victoria Crosses for shooting men who had already given themselves up.

No part of the German army was ever demoralized. They always fought well, and the Canadian boys who fought them would be among the first to admit it. I once saw a German machine-gunner with his leg torn half off and blood streaming down all over his face from a wound in the head desperately trying to get his machine gun back in operation, while the other four members of his crew lay dead and dying in the shell hole beside him.

While our regiment, as a whole, suffered fewer casualties during the Passchendaele massacre of 1917 than it had the previous year on the Somme front, where our whole regiment was wiped out in just one day, the Signal Corps (of which I was a member) lost well over 50 percent of its complement. Being without reserves for replacement, the few of us left were so worn out and exhausted from overwork and lack of sleep that proper maintenance of communication became just about impossible.

I recall one of the many generals at Aldershot telling us just a few days before shipping us off to Egypt and the Dardanelles that, although our rifles were new and much more powerful than those they had replaced, we would probably have been just as well off with the old ones. He said that the only need we would ever be likely to have for rifles in battle would be as handles to hold our bayonets. I saw many hundreds of dead men both during and after an attack, but never one that had been killed or even wounded by a bayonet.

While I never saw a dead German soldier who had died from bayonet wounds, I once saw four whose throats had been slit wide open by one or more bayonets, but there was overwhelming evidence to prove that all four of them had been dead for at least eight hours, perhaps longer, prior to having their throats cut by a gang of depraved, despicable hoodlums — degenerates of which the British army had a full quota, particularly so during the last two years of the war. The bottom of the barrel began to show: Sir Douglas was taking the few of us that still survived the Ypres and Passchendaele massacres and gambling us away so fast [because] he was desperate for manpower. To fill the demand, newly convicted criminals and presently incarcerated ones were given the option of either serving their time in prison or serving the army in France for the war's duration.

I first saw those four unfortunate butchered enemy soldiers while on my way up to a company outpost to relieve one of our front-line signallers, who had been on duty there for almost forty-eight hours. Three of the dead Germans were lying in the same large shell hole: one was face up, another two face down. The fourth was alone in a shell hole nearby, lying on his side with his knees drawn up until they almost touched his chin. Neither he nor any of the other three showed any signs of bayonet wounds, but when I stopped by there on my way back the following morning, all four were facing skyward with gaps in their throats so deep, wide, and ugly that their heads were all but severed from their bodies. *My God,* I kept thinking, *how could one human being do such an awful thing to another?* Was this a part of the "justice of our cause" that Sir Douglas and his top brass generals were continually spouting off about? I reported what I had seen to brigade headquarters and was told that they already knew about it and it was being investigated and taken care of — meaning "don't bother us with such petty things."

British newspapers and the official military bulletins from Haig's headquarters would have the public believe that British soldiers were longing to be sent out on patrols and trench raids. On the contrary, all of the soldiers I ever knew and talked with dreaded such missions. Like myself and my friends, they wanted no part in them.

That silent but powerful thing we call our conscience is not always easy to follow, and frequently tends to get us into as much or more trouble as we had hoped it would keep us out of. As a signaller I was obliged to work both night and day. Emergencies could occur at any time, and usually did. Our telegraph and telephone lines were forever being cut or disrupted by shell fire and the signallers were constantly being killed or wounded while out in open terrain trying to repair them. Mud and quagmire were never less than ankle to half-leg deep in and around any part of the Ypres Salient, especially so during this, the rainy season. Our casualties in the signal corp, except in periods of open battle, were at least 30 to 50 percent higher than those of any other front-line troops.

So many nights when we had just got through another of those horrible days all in one piece, we were wet, cold, and ready to drop from sheer exhaustion. Then a call would come through from one or another of our front-line units, stating that it had lost its last or next-to-last signaller and one of us must hurry out to take his place. I cannot recall one single night when I got more than two hours sleep at any one time during front-line duty.

Wading through that dismal, devastated quagmire and total desolation, either on my way to a company outpost or searching for broken communication lines, with shells flying overhead and death and destruction everywhere about me, I suffered periods of gloom and self-pity. Even more often I accused and reproached myself for having been such a sensitive, soft-hearted idiot in voluntarily giving up the easiest and most comfortable assignment, only to be found in or near any part of the front-line trenches.

My lawyer once told me that any time he had a court case he considered to be weak, he always tried to place as many men of Irish origin on the jury as possible. He said that Irishmen have a tendency to picture themselves as being in a similar situation as that of the accused and their sympathy was always for the underdog, and only in cases where there was absolutely no doubt and their conscience gave them no alternative would they bring in a verdict of guilty. Even then, it was usually followed with a strong recommendation for leniency. I am not Irish, but the same feelings of empathy applied. I never could feel less sorry for the German boys I saw lying dead in one shell hole than I did for our boys lying dead in another. Some of those ugly blood- and water-filled shell craters that our telegraph lines crossed over or ran close to, contained the bloated bodies of both friend and foe alike, floating around side by side. It was as though they had purposely willed it that way; as if they had agreed that since they were no longer permitted to live as friends, at peace with each other in life, they would seek both peace and reconciliation in death.

On the afternoon of August 16, I received word from my signal officer at battalion headquarters, advising me that as there were no other signallers left that he could send to help me through the night, I would just have to get along as best I could in taking care of communication between D Company and battalion headquarters. He would have to take care of headquarters himself or help to do so, as two of his signallers had been seriously wounded the night before while out making repairs to the lines, and his last remaining two would have to stand by to replace them.

D Company, situated way out in what was now more or less a part of no man's land, held one of the German blockhouses, a machine-gun fort, which, after suffering very heavy losses in both killed and wounded, we had infiltrated and captured the previous night, taking the four or five enemy crew members as prisoners of war. Those machine-gun forts, or pillboxes as the infantrymen were quick to dub them (because of their peculiar shape), were not just bulletproof, they were shell proof, and like von Lossberg,[2] who conceived and planned them, and his technicians, who located and constructed them, they were practically indestructible.

If one or more of our luxury-living strategists had been capable of providing our troops with a similar kind of overall defence system, half or more of the million boys whose bones were left to rot in the Somme and Flanders mud would have made it back. This is not just an opinion of one common, front-line signaller, but the firm conviction of the thousands of thinking men and their company officers who fought and suffered with them.

About an hour or so after receiving my orders, I gathered my equipment and, after waiting as long as I dared for darkness to set in to hide me from the enemy's machine-gunners and snipers, I began my short but perilous journey through the ankle-deep mud and scummed-over, water-filled shell holes in the direction of the newly captured, sparsely defended blockhouse. Patrolling and inspecting our telegraph lines on the way, I arrived at the blockhouse about forty minutes later. After setting up my equipment and receiving an O.K. signal from battalion headquarters, being very tired from overwork and lack of sleep, I stretched out on the concrete floor of the pillbox, beside the set, for what I hoped would be a nice long rest, but within the hour, the company captain was shaking me awake again. He was much concerned by the reports from his listening patrol, who warned him that the Germans appeared to be preparing for a mass counterattack and he was most anxious to get in touch with battalion headquarters, so that the troops on both flanks could be alerted.

The Germans had now begun to increase their artillery fire to some extent, and in all probability, that is what gave the listening patrol boys the idea that a German counterattack was likely, as there were no attacks that night, and judging from what I saw a few hours later, I doubt if there were any large-scale attacks on that sector of the front for many days after.

The telegraph set, which had been operating perfectly less than an hour before when I lay down to rest, was now quite dead, indicating that somewhere between the pillbox and battalion headquarters, the lines had been cut or disrupted by shell fire. Due to our battalion's recent success in forcing the enemy back a few hundred feet in that particular location, we no longer had any communication trench [to service this new front line], which, in addition to being some protection for the troops and supplies in transit, was also used to conceal and protect our telegraph lines. We were now compelled to lay the wires over wide-open terrain, and, as a result, they were constantly being cut by exploding shells. To make matters worse, the new type of phillorphone we were now using[3] called for two wires to complete the circuit instead of just a single wire and an earth or ground pin, as used on the old-type set. Both work and time in making repairs had more than doubled — and so had the risk of being killed or wounded.

The company captain, much disturbed at not being able to get in immediate touch with battalion headquarters, ordered me to get repairs made right away. There was a kind of unwritten law at the front, or at least there was in our regiment, that if it could be prevented, a man must not be sent out alone on a mission of this nature. This was particularly so anywhere in or around no man's land. That way, if there were two men and one had the misfortune of being shot or disabled, the other could give him emergency treatment and perhaps, as so often happened, carry him on his back to safety. If, however, he considered the injured man's condition too serious for that kind of transportation, he could later guide or direct the stretcher-bearers to the wounded man's location.

I suggested to the captain that if he loaned me one of his men, we would then take his message direct to battalion headquarters and make repairs to the telegraph lines on the way back. The captain was sorry, he said, but being in such a tight spot with so few men left to defend the outpost and expecting to be attacked at any moment, he dared not weaken his defences further by sending one of his men to help me. Moreover, maintenance and care of communications was the Signal Corps' responsibility, not his. Under and during normal conditions, this might have been the correct attitude to take, but with so few of us left, nothing was normal anymore, and considering the circumstances, I felt that he was being rather unreasonable. But right or wrong, a common soldier dared not question or argue with an officer, and although [I felt] rather bitter and resentful at his remarks, I have always regretted not having thanked him for wishing me good luck when I left, for I was never to see him again.

On my way back to England almost two years later, I was informed of how the gallant captain, with several of his courageous men, had died in a fierce hand-to-hand battle on another sector of the front a year or so later. One of his men, seriously wounded in the same battle, who came to visit me in a St. John's hospital almost three years later,[4] told me all about how the captain had accused himself of letting me go out all alone that night, and on the following night, he and a couple of his men had spent considerable time searching in and around the numerous shell craters trying to locate my body. Due to the fact that no enemy attacks or patrols had been reported for miles on either flank that night, no one suspected that there was a possibility of my being taken prisoner. Having found my pliers where I had left them after making the last splice in the telegraph wire, they took it for granted that I had been blown to pieces by one of the heavy-type shells that had made such an awful mess in that vicinity.

On my return home, my mother showed me two letters as part of her most prized possessions — one from the company captain and one from my signal officer. Like most letters written about people supposed to have passed on, [it was] very complimentary but grossly exaggerated. But my mother, like most mothers the world over I suspect, believed every word of it, and I have always been grateful to both officers for being so thoughtful and considerate, those letters being of much comfort to her during the many months she thought me dead.

About two hundred yards from the pillbox, I located and repaired the first break in the lines. Then, with the wires sliding through the crook of each arm, I groped my way on toward battalion headquarters. The Germans were sending over quite a few whiz-bang-type shells. It could not be described as heavy; however, the shell holes from previous bombardments were as numerous as fleas on a dog. In most cases, the shell holes were either lip to lip or overlapped each other. Quite a few contained the bodies of both British and German soldiers from the early morning's fighting. The wounded, both German and British, had already been taken care of, but owing to the risk involved in gathering them for burial, most of the dead would have to remain where they fell for the time being.

About one-third of the distance to battalion headquarters, I found the second (and what I hoped would be the last) broken line. When I had pulled both ends together over the shell hole in order to make the splice, I was obliged to straddle one of the three German bodies lying there. I had just got finished and was about to withdraw when I heard the swish and rumbling noise made only by one of the heavier-type shells as it speeds through the atmosphere. From the many past experiences, I could judge by the sound that it would come dangerously close to where I was standing. Throwing myself down on the body of the dead German boy whose number had been called earlier in the morning, I held fast. Immediately, there was a terrific, frightening explosion, which knocked me unconscious, but not for long. As I came to, I could neither see nor hear a thing, but my sense of smell assured me that I must still be alive, since the awful stench from the torn and mangled bodies was beyond description.

Considerable time passed before I somehow managed to pull myself together enough to find out just how badly hurt I was. What appeared to be the muscle, or part of it, was hanging from the upper part of my left arm. There were numerous cuts and bruises on my hands and on the back of my neck, none of which appeared to be too serious, however. My steel helmet was crushed and shapeless, yet the only injury to my head was a couple of medium-size bumps. My legs showed no sign of injury, but when I tried to stand up and take a step forward, I came very close to falling flat on my face. It was then that I discovered that the lower half of my back was numb and lifeless.

After what seemed like an hour or more, my head began to clear. I could see that a large new crater had been formed, the outer rim of which overlapped the hole I was in to about half its width. One of the German bodies had completely disappeared, and that of the second blown into bits and pieces and scattered all over on my side of the crater. The body of the boy underneath me was still intact, and although it was still rather dark, I could see the outline of his features quite clearly. He was a handsome, clean-cut youth, not a day over eighteen years of age. Even the wound from the bullet, or bullets, that had killed him was not visible, and he did not appear to be dead. He looked more like a weary, overtired boy who had just lain down to sleep, but had forgotten how to wake up.

I was no stranger to fear, having been shelled and shot at [in] the Dardanelles and twice wounded in France. Nevertheless, the realization that I could no longer walk and may be compelled to remain in this awful shell crater to die had me scared just about out of my wits. My arm was bleeding freely and I was much concerned lest I pass out and bleed to death before being able to do anything to prevent it.

Although there seemed to be no feeling in the lower part of my back on touching it with my fingers, the pain from somewhere inside was becoming almost unbearable. Mustering every ounce of strength I possessed, I somehow managed to wrap a field dressing around the upper part of my arm and, by using the bayonet borrowed from the dead German boy's scabbard as a lever, I twisted it as tightly as I could bear and succeeded in reducing the flow of blood to a minimum. As I lay there, flat on my stomach and helpless, I found it impossible to keep from looking at the dead German boy's handsome face, which appeared to be so calm and peaceful, as though he was content and pleased to be done with it all. Despite the fact that I was suffering severe mental anguish and [was] filled with a deep, terrifying fear at being so near to death myself, I sensed a great surge of pity and sympathy and perhaps a little guilt.

I never could explain why, that now my last hope of ever reaching my friends at the outpost was gone, I no longer felt the least sense of fear. It could have been shock due to the sudden and unexpected surprise in the turn of events, but surrounded as I was by those armed enemy soldiers, all I could think of was what a stupid fool I had been. If only in circumstances of this kind, we could exchange a little hindsight for foresight. Now that I had placed myself into this incredible situation and there was absolutely nothing I could do about it, what I should have done was now crystal clear. If, instead of taking the shorter and more dangerous route over the open terrain to the pillbox, I had continued on toward battalion headquarters, it is almost certain that I would have either made it on my own or been rescued by my friends, and by now might have been well on my way to what every front-line, trench-weary trooper constantly dreams of: a nice warm bath and a clean soft bed — perhaps a nice friendly nurse.

For some reason or other, the calm and serene features of that dead German boy reminded me of the 23rd Psalm,[5] and I have never since thought of one without thinking of the other. I wondered about his loved ones back in Germany or if he would mind if he knew that his bayonet was being used to save the life of an enemy and not as it was meant — to take it.

I doubt very much if he ever wished or wanted to use the cursed thing at any time, nor would there be need or reason for such cruel and inhumane weapons to kill and murder whole generations of young men and teenage boys like him and me if both our governments had been made up of good common-sense statesmen who were willing to compromise rather than threaten — men with a deep, sincere, and humane consideration for the less fortunate — men less greedy, covetous, and uncompromising — men with compassion and pity for the millions of youths on both sides of the line who were compelled to shoot and bayonet each other to death for no known reason, except that they were told to do so by some fool politicians and incompetent diplomats and the military-minded war-mongering autocrats, [and told] that it was the right and patriotic thing to do.

The only thing right about it was the right of the establishments, the right for kings, princes, bluebloods, and war lords, to continue without the least inconvenience or danger to themselves, to live in lavish luxury, while the millions of their lesser bred countrymen such as this young dead German boy and I, who had never seen or heard of each other before, were forced out into the knee-deep Flanders blood-drenched mud, murdered and crucified so that they — the bluebloods, the kaisers, and the kings — could gain more prestige, power, and fame and add more of the so-called glory and grandeur to their already great and mighty imperial empires.

After lying there for an hour, perhaps two, sick with both pain and fear, I determined that in some way, somehow, I must make it to the nearest large- or medium-sized shell hole, away from the awful smell and stench of the mangled German bodies. I first tried rolling my body in a kind of hoop-wise motion, but the pain in my back was just too much. Then, while still lying flat on my stomach, I discovered that I could pull my knees up under the lower part of my body with considerable ease. How it was possible to use my hips to crawl and yet not be able to walk, I did not know, but it also did not matter. It must have taken the better part of five minutes to reach the nearest large-sized shell hole not more than fifty feet away, but the realization that I could move forward again, even at this slow pace, and may yet have time to make it all the way back to the outpost and safety under the cover of darkness inspired new hope. Here, in this new shell hole, which held no dead bodies and less of the horrible sickening stench, I began to feel much better and to think more clearly.

The dread of being left out there all alone to die had now completely subsided, and I was determined to make it all the way to the outpost before the break of day, otherwise I would be compelled to remain in one of those horrible shell craters until the following night. After rearranging the bandage on my arm as best I could, dabbing some iodine on as many of the cuts as I could reach, [and] dispensing with all of my equipment, except my water bottle and gas mask, I headed back in the direction of the pillbox, which was my second-to-biggest mistake of the entire war (my first and biggest occurred way back in 1914 when I volunteered to become involved in the first place). Using my injured arm to help support the upper part of my body, the going was extremely slow and painful, but I was making progress and my spirit and morale rose with every yard I covered.

Two hours or so later and about halfway back to the pillbox, I was greeted with just that one harsh, challenging word, "Halt" (which means the same thing in both languages), and within seconds, I was surrounded by a patrol of German soldiers. Apparently, this was not going to be one of my luckier days.

I don't know if those German soldiers were scared or not, but they should have been as it must have taken plenty of guts to have manoeuvred so close inside our newly captured outpost. They did have the advantage of knowing every foot of the terrain, having lost it only the morning before, after occupying it since the beginning of the war. All six of them, including the officer in charge, were very young men, and except for that one word, "Halt," none of them spoke or understood English. I am inclined to think that taking me prisoner was just a coincidence. I think their real purpose was to gather information regarding our strength and to determine the space between outposts. They might have found some of their own wounded men still alive in one or more of the numerous shell holes.

When I saw the young officer looking at the dead German boy's bayonet that I was using to tighten the tourniquet on my arm, I thought perhaps he might misunderstand how I came by it. I felt rather pleased that I had never made it a practice to accept or take watches or other personal belongings from either alive or dead German soldiers, as some front-line troops felt they had every right to do after winning a battle. Thankfully, neither the officer nor any of his men acted unfriendly. In fact, I could not have been treated more kindly by the boys in my own regiment. My biggest surprise came when they took the extra time to rebandage and apply a new tourniquet to my arm, as each minute's delay increased the risk of their being shot or captured. The lieutenant and two of his heavier-built men spelled each other in carrying me piggyback all the way across no man's land.

Thirty minutes or so later, we were in a deep, huge dugout beneath one of their front-line trenches, where the lieutenant, after making a short phone call, handed me a big coffee mug half filled with a greyish-white liquid, which I later learned was called schnapps, but to me, it tasted like turpentine and burned like lye. When he saw how my stomach rebelled, he let out with a jolly laugh, took it back, and drank it down in one short gulp as though it was just water. He then had one of his men fetch me the one and only cup of coffee that I would be served in almost two years.

A few minutes later, two other soldiers came in with a stretcher and I was taken back to their casualty clearing station. Before leaving, although the only German I knew were a few dirty, uncomplimentary phrases frequently shouted back and forth across no man's land, I did try (and I think, to some extent succeeded) in conveying to them some of the gratitude I felt for their very kind and friendly treatment. All six of them waved me goodbye, and although I did not know it then, I would meet very few people in Germany (or in German-occupied France for at least the first half of my sixteen months' internment) who would treat me as kindly as they had. They were considerate, humane, and courageous, and it has always been my sincere wish that they survived the remainder of the war and returned safely to friends and loved ones.

From the casualty clearing station, where I was given temporary medical attention, I was placed in an ambulance filled with wounded German soldiers and taken to the German-occupied Belgian city of Ghent, which I surmised served as general headquarters for that sector of the Flanders front. One of the badly wounded soldiers died during the trip.

It was here I had to match wits with a general, or at least I supposed he was a general. I have never been sure, but judging from all the medals and decorations he was wearing, he could have been the Crown Prince. He was a handsome man and no doubt a very intelligent one. He was also the most domineering, arrogant, and tyrannical individual that it has ever been my misfortune to encounter. Despite his intelligence and ability, there were intervals during that interrogation in which he ranted and raved equal to any lunatic that ever wore a straightjacket. He asked me questions that could not be correctly answered by more than a dozen or so of our top brass at the War Office in London. He wanted to know how many British ships were being sunk each week by German submarines and the number of divisions on our sector of the front and in reserve. He was well aware, of course, that I possessed no such information.

Nevertheless, common sense warned me that these questions were not being fired at me without reason. If he could catch me lying about things he knew that I had little or no knowledge of, he would have a much better idea of what to expect when he got around to pumping me about some of the vital information that the signallers like me possess, such as the number of men still left in the regiment after our recent offensive, reserves, and reinforcements. Fortunately, I had already anticipated such questions. I had also made up my mind that once I had given an answer, I would stick with it come hell or high water. So when he asked me how many men were still left in the battalion after our recent battle, I did not exaggerate too much because, like all previous battles where our men were compelled to wade through a foot or more of mud against those well-concealed and protected German death-spitting machine guns, our casualties were always frightfully heavy regardless as to whether the attack succeeded or failed.

To offset the high percentage of casualties, however, in case he was thinking that now would be a good time to counterattack, I told him that about four hundred reinforcements had joined our unit the previous afternoon. For this, he slapped me across the face, calling me a "dirty lying English pig," yelling and ranting like some wild Indian about to take off on the warpath, while strutting back and forth across the office floor. He swore he would have me locked up without food or water and no doctor would be permitted to ease my pain until, as he put it, I came to my senses.

Except for the cup of coffee given me that morning by the kind-hearted lieutenant, I had not eaten since early the day before. As for my senses, they did not fail me once all through that terrible interrogation, perhaps because never before did I have such desperate need of them. On my refusal to deny the accuracy of the number of reinforcements I had given him, he posed as if to kick me, but threw a half-pitcher of ice water in my face instead, as I lay there helpless on the stretcher. I never could be both scared and angry at the same time, and now that I was good and mad, this big sword-rattling Prussian did not frighten me anymore. I determined that the only way he would ever know as to whether I was telling the truth or not would be the hard way — by counterattacking our line — and if and when he did, I wished and hoped that some of those imaginary four hundred reinforcements would have materialized to give him a very hot reception.

Regardless of any threats or torture, which I felt sure he was quite capable of inflicting, I would never knowingly part with any information that could in any way be useful to him or harmful to my friends and comrades still sweating it out back there, in those wet, cold foxholes and bits of stinking blood-soaked trenches, exposed to all the most deadly and powerful weapons ever invented.

I was not at all surprised when he later correctly named the two divisions situated on our right and left, which I had previously refused to do. In fact, he knew as much or more about many things on our side of the line than I did. Nevertheless, it was quite evident that if I went along with him on the things he already knew, I could quite easily be trapped later into confirming those of which he was only guessing at.

I asked him why, if he knew all these particulars, he kept on grilling me. Instead of getting all riled up again, this officer began to act quite human, withdrawing a folder from one of his file cabinets, which I later suspected was an old list of ships from Lloyd's Register, probably obtained before the war. He must have named as many as fifty or more ships including three of Britain's most powerful battleships, all of which (according to him) had either been sunk by German U-boats during the previous three months, or so badly damaged as to be no longer fit for sea. It was public knowledge, of course, that some of those ships had been sunk. The British Admiralty had already admitted the loss.

I have no idea how good he was as a general, but as an actor, he would have been superb. The author of *Doctor Jekyll and Mr. Hyde* must have known or had such a character in mind when he wrote his famous play. In his new role as a politician and statesman, I listened for a full twenty minutes or more to one of the most ambitious political schemes ever conceived. As I listened, I became convinced that not only did he believe every word of what he was spouting, but the possibility of Germany not winning the war had never occurred to him. He sketched a complete outline of the elaborate plans made, or in the making, by the kaiser's imperial government and general staff, of what both Europe and America would be like after Germany had won the war.

It was late in the afternoon when the general quit quizzing me, too late, I was told, to be admitted to hospital that night, as I must first be deloused and given a bath, which meant that I would just have to suffer until the men detailed for that kind of work returned in the morning. I spent the whole of that night in a cold, isolated shed with just some dirty straw strewn over the damp concrete floor as bedding. The pain in my back was near to unbearable and kept me awake all through the night. Early the next morning, two civilians came in with a stretcher, took me over to the main building, and gave me a bath. They offered me some food, but I was just too sick and disheartened to eat. The nice warm water soon had me feeling a whole lot better, however, and helped much to ease the pain in my back. It also helped to revive some of my lost morale.

The doctor who examined me at the hospital was both sympathetic and humane, for which I have always remembered him. He ordered immediate surgery for my arm. Whether he performed the operation or not, I don't know, but whoever it was did an excellent job. It felt so good and wonderful to be clean and warm and resting in a nice soft bed again after all the frightful months of mud, blood, and grime. I came very close to forgetting that I was in enemy country.

One day, about a week after being admitted, the doctor, who spoke only German, had an English-speaking Belgian priest come in to tell me that I need not worry further about my back, as the disc joints, which had been twisted or dislocated by the shell fragments that had hit me, were now properly readjusted and would be quite well again within a week or two. My arm would take much longer to heal, but in his opinion, there would be no permanent injury. This was good news indeed, and I thanked the priest for coming to see me and requested that he convey to the doctor and his staff my deep and sincere gratitude for treating me so well. The doctor acknowledged my thanks with a smile and "… ja, ja, so, so, Englander."

I began to think about God, war, and how a German doctor had treated me so effectively, as I lay wondering about what lay ahead. All through our training period in Britain, prior to embarking for Egypt and the Dardanelles, attending church service on Sunday was compulsory. Nobody, unless sick or assigned to other duty, was exempt. Being a skeptic, agnostic, or atheist was no excuse. We were given a choice of denominational churches, but, unless we were prepared to forfeit all of our off-duty evenings by being confined to our quarters during the following week or spending a week in the pokey if we refused a second time (and as many of us were already in enough trouble for minor fractions of the so-called King's Rules), we usually went.

But, for me and for most of the other boys who had been born and raised in religious homes, it required few enforced Sunday parades to the many beautiful churches to convince us we were wasting our time. If what those ordained men of the cloth were bellowing from those magnificently chisel-carved pulpits to a captive audience of four or five hundred young men — many of whom were about to die — was the kind of religion that they actually believed to be the will and intent of a loving, forgiving, and merciful God, our commanding officer would have done us a far greater service by permitting us to remain in our quarters on Sundays to play poker or a few games of "Crown and Anchor."

Kill, demolish, destroy with few exceptions — that was the main theme or topic of most sermons preached by the majority of those so-called disciples of Christ. These were supposedly men of culture and refinement who had spent more years in good schools and universities than well over 90 percent of their captive colonial audience had been privileged to spend weeks, or even days. They acted and sounded far more hostile and bloodthirsty toward the German people than any of the old sergeant majors and bayonet instructors over on the drill grounds. They were supposed to be followers of Jesus — the man of love, peace, and compassion. They seldom, if ever, mentioned his name. Not once, to my knowledge, did any of them speak of spiritual matters, which could have aided and strengthened the simple but deep-rooted faith that most of our island people had inherited and so firmly and sincerely believed in down through the centuries. This was a faith that had sustained and encouraged them to overcome so many long years of poverty, hardship, and disaster.

Although we received little or no spiritual food for our souls from any of those compulsory church parades, we sure got our bellies full of patriotism, nationalism, flag waving, and imperialism. Already, according to those apostles of the church, we were heroes who had done our good and great mother country a grand and noble service by voluntarily coming so far from our homeland to help fight and destroy her wicked and depraved enemies. Because we would be fighting for truth, justice, and the deliverance of the poor, enslaved, and tortured Belgian people, God would fight along with us and great would be our reward.

*And great shall be your reward,* those very imperialistic churchmen assured us. Some reward. After years of being sent like sheep to the slaughter, by those "beyond the danger zone" autocrats whom none of us had ever seen or ever would while the war was still on, the thousands who were not killed outright died of their wounds or [were] mentally disabled for life after more than four, long dreadful years of horror, misery, torment, and fear and were compelled to leave our homes and loved ones again within a year or less to wander all over the North American continent in search of work. In order to keep body and soul together, we were often obliged to accept the most menial kind of work, work that even the poorest and most destitute welfare residents felt it beneath their dignity to accept or perform.

God would reward us, the preachers assured us. Well, perhaps they were right. Maybe God gave us exactly what we deserved, or might even have overpaid us for the kind of work that we were compelled to perform in the Flanders blood-drenched mud. After all, we were breaking just about every one of his Ten Commandments, including the one that says, Thou Shalt Not Kill. But if such was God's reward for the poor bloody front-line infantrymen, who were given no choice or alternative other than to shoot or bayonet to death the thousands of other young men whom they had never seen or heard of before, why did he show such a vast amount of preferential treatment when he got around to rewarding the men at the top?

Of the ten volunteers from [Botwood] and its surrounding neighbourhood who joined the regiment when I did early in the war … the first two [had] died in the Dardanelles in 1915 — one was shot through the head by a sniper, the other blown to shreds by an exploding shell. Two others were killed during the Battle of the Somme a year later, and five of us were wounded in the same battle. The only one not wounded on that tragic 1st of July, 1916, morning was killed on the Cambrai front the following year. We had all served in the Dardanelles before coming to France. Three of us had returned to France for a second time after recovering from wounds and one for a third time. The last two of the seven to die were machine-gunned to death in the so-called Third Battle of Ypres, while so desperately struggling to cross the flaming inferno of no man's land through the devastated blood-reddened quagmire. Only three of us survived to return home.

Ten boys, all under twenty years of age, from England's most neglected colony. I doubt if there were another ten boys in the whole British Empire with less to protect or defend or with less cause to fight and die for their so-called king and country. I doubt if the entire worth of our whole village would cover or equal the cost of two of England's long-range field guns, and because our people lacked the means to pay for our tuition, six of our number attended school for only two or three terms. The other four, including me, fared very little better. What little education we did have was, for the most part, self-taught. But what did the sirs, lords, dukes, and other autocratic members of the Whitehall and Westminster establishment care whether we were educated or not. Uneducated men could shoot or stop bullets every bit as well as college professors, and according to the official casualty list, we stopped a whole lot more than our share.

I was discharged from the Ghent hospital about six or seven weeks after being admitted, having been treated as well as any prisoner of war should ever expect to be. Early in October, I was transferred to Brussels, where, after another two weeks of convalescence, I was again moved on to a town named Dendermonde.[6] The prisoner-of-war camp there appeared to be a huge clearing station, where prisoners from the various sectors of the British front were being held until such time as they would be needed to join working gangs elsewhere. I never did get to find out much about the place, however. A few hours after my arrival there, I was handed a piece of black war bread and, together with a few other prisoners, escorted by two soldiers with fixed bayonets all the way back across town to the railway station and pushed into one of the cattle cars standing at the siding.

Those cattle cars, stinking exactly like cow stalls, were filled with prisoners from Australia, New Zealand, the British Isles, and two or three from Tasmania — 158 in all. None of us had any knowledge of where we were going, and the miserable hard-hearted guards were so arrogant and mean that all they would say was "nein," "nix," and "Englander du schwein."[7] Some of the prisoners, having heard rumours of secret prison slave camps behind the German trenches, were much concerned lest we were on our way to one of them instead of being sent to a registered POW camp back in Germany. The difference in the two types of camps could be (and, in our case, was) all the difference between paradise and hell.

It took two full days and three nights to reach our destination, not more than 120 to 190 miles from where we started. We did not travel at night, and for some reason or other known only to the guards and crew, we spent most of the days pulling in and out of railway sidings and depots, and in all that time (two days and three nights), except for the fifth of black bread handed us before leaving Dendermonde, we were never given another bite of food. They did, however, pass pails of water around at some of the numerous stops along the way.

Sometimes, when the train pulled in at small village depots or nearby sidings, the Belgian people, mostly children, would come as close as they dared and throw us some apples, but as the plank siding on the cattle cars were spaced very little farther apart than the width of the diameter of an apple, most of the apples squashed or dropped to the ground on contact with the planks. When the children tried coming close enough to push the apples through the openings, the miserable stone-hearted guards would threaten and chase them away with their bayonets. Poor kids — they were so sorry and disappointed at not being able to help us more that some of the little girls actually broke down and cried. Most of them looked as though they were not getting enough food themselves, or at least not enough of the right kind.

Looking through the openings between the plank siding after the officer had left and the guards had cooled off, I could see and sense by the light and glow in the faces of those Belgian people, both young and old, that the singing of their beloved and glorious anthem, instigated and inspired by a cattle train load of dirty, cold, and hungry Allied prisoners, had set them on fire and would forever be for them (as it would for my fellow prisoners and me) one of the very few thrills of exaltation experienced in one's lifetime.

Early on the morning of the third day, our train arrived at or near the town of Rethel,[8] in enemy-occupied France, and from the large number of guards lined up at the depot, we realized that this, or somewhere nearby, was the end of the line. What we did not realize was that for many of us, it would also turn out to be the end of the road. Some of the prisoners, having lain on the cold, damp car floors for such a long time, were now so ill and weak from hunger and chill they could no longer take care of themselves, and some of the other prisoners were ordered by the *Field Webel*[9] to carry them to the lorries that were waiting to take us to the work site, which was a considerable distance west of Rethel and within sound of the guns.

When the wind was in a certain direction, we were never under shellfire, although we did hear of some British prisoners who had been sent close enough to the firing line to be within artillery range of the long-distance guns, supposedly in retaliation for something the British had done to some of their prisoners. I have no proof of this, however, and I am inclined to doubt it, because, while there were individual officers on both sides who would not have hesitated in giving such an order had they been permitted to do so, I feel quite sure that neither Marshal von Hindenburg or General Ludendorff, both of whom were very well thought of and respected by friend and foe alike, would not have tolerated such inhumane behaviour. Generals who made up the kaiser's high command in the First World War were gentlemen, while most of those who made up Hitler's in the Second World War were not.

This *Field Webel,* as they are called in Germany, would be in charge of us from now on. He was an inconceivable monster — brutal, cruel, and evil, lacking in humanity; ruthless, merciless, and without one redeemable quality. He was about fifty years of age. Two of his sons had been killed on the British sector of the Western Front the previous year, and he treated each and every one of us as though we had personally and deliberately gone out and murdered them.

It took two or more hours to reach the camp, and what a camp it was. The prisoners' quarters consisted of an old deserted French barn with a long, narrow lean-to type shack adjoining each end, with mud floors. Much of the roof was wide open to the heavens, and the cracks in the walls were almost as wide as the doors. The straw used for bedding was always wet and cold due to the rains and snow coming through the numerous openings, particularly so when the wind blew, which seemed to be most of the time. The whole miserable ghostlike place was enclosed with the old familiar rusty barbed wire forming a barricade twelve or fifteen feet high. This was indeed an island of lost souls.

After being without food now for two full days and three nights, we were fed some kind of swill, made up of unwashed potatoes exactly as they came out of the ground, *mangelwurzel,*[10] sauerkraut, nettle tree, and

God knows what, all cooked together in a huge barrel-sized iron kettle. It looked a little like soup, but smelled and tasted like bilge water. With this awful mess, we were each given one-eighth of a loaf of black war bread. This was to be our daily ration for as long as we were there, except that on the following day and for all the days thereafter, we were given the piece of bread when we left for work at daybreak each morning and the horrible-smelling swill when we returned from work each night. Not once did we see meat of any kind, but the smell of it being cooked and prepared for the *Field Webel* and his guards in their kitchen nearby came nigh to driving us all insane with the longing, craving, and yearning for some of it.

It would be a complete waste of time to talk of anything except food to a starving man. His mind could not absorb any other subject. Sex or the desire for women has long since disappeared. He is no longer interested in religion, politics, world affairs, peace, or war. Nothing, unless in some way connected with food, has meaning. Not even the loss of a loved one or something as dreadful as a worldwide disaster would be drastic enough to take his mind from the constant and continual craving for something to eat, nor does he think in terms of big thick juicy porterhouse steaks, prime rib roasts, or centre cut pork chops. These are luxuries he wished for when he was just hungry. Starving, he thinks only of crusts of bread, fats, drippings, and all the precious scraps of food being thrown in the many garbage cans by the very fortunate people who prepared and cooked more than they could eat.

Those of us still able to drag ourselves to work at the end of the second month at that horrible slave prison camp had lost a full third of our normal body weight.[11] Draped in our old, dirty, torn, and tattered uniforms, which were now several sizes too big and, in most cases, without shoes, we looked like a parade of sleepwalking skeletons. One of the prisoners, a member of one of England's guard regiments whom I first saw on the cattle train from Dendermonde, was tall (about six foot one or two) and well-constructed with handsome features. He stood out among most of the other boys like a Greek god. Now, less than three months later, he still looked different from the rest of us, but no longer for his stature or good looks — the change in his appearance since I had first seen him was dreadful. The flesh on his face had all but disappeared, leaving folds of sagging skin. The cheekbones appeared to have protruded to more than twice the normal size. His head looked to be two feet long and all out of proportion. He was as thin as a beanpole, ghostlike, and actually ugly to look upon. But his morale and determination to survive and return home to England was indomitable. I wish I could say that he made it, but, unfortunately, he died a month or so later.

At daybreak each morning, we were lined up in military formation and divided into separate slave gangs. Some of us were sent to unload cement, angle iron, planks, etc., from railway cars used in the construction of the big new Siegfried super-defence line, better known to the British as the Hindenburg Line.[12] Some gangs were compelled to take an active part in actual building of the gun forts. Other gangs constructed dams across the canal and in the low-lying terrain from one to several hundred yards out in front of the gun forts. This work consisted of cutting down trees (mostly willows), which, together with the limbs and brush, were squeezed into bundles with the aid of levers and pressure chains. They were then fastened with wire or strong cord and placed in and around the low-lying swampland, in the style of a beaver dam. Some of the prisoners were compelled to stand almost waist-high in the ice-cold water for hours each day, laying the bundles of willows in place.

During the first week or two at that horrible slave camp, we conversed much with each other and had much to talk about, coming from the many and varied parts of the Empire. There were so many different and interesting points of view on just about every subject and topic discussed that some kind of friendly argument was going on most of the time, but as the dreary, cold, hungry days came and went and hope faded, we became almost as strangers to each other again. The constant longing and yearning for food caused everything else to become insignificant. We thought of nothing else all through the day, and when we became weary and exhausted enough for our empty rattling stomachs to permit sleep, we dreamed of it all night.

These dams were designed to flood all the low-lying countryside, thereby making it that much more difficult for the Allies to break through. With the Germans' new shell-proof, concrete machine-gun placements on the higher ground at the rear, very few men would be required to defend and hold this sector of the front. This would thereby relieve as many as ten or more divisions from this part of the front for service elsewhere.

About two weeks after our arrival at that horrible God-forsaken camp, one of the prisoners who had been too ill to walk from the train at Rethel died and two or three others were seriously ill. The guards kept promising that a doctor would be sent in, but no doctor came, and a couple of weeks later, two others died of pneumonia. As far as we knew then, only the English-hating, unapproachable *Field Webel* could speak or understand English. The guards, or at least some of them, appeared to be sympathetic, but apparently there was little or nothing they could do to help us. No doubt, the *Field Webel*, who they seemed to fear almost as much as the prisoners did, was being kept well informed, and, as we found out later, we were receiving the kind of treatment that he had planned for us from the beginning.

Being near enough to the front to sometimes hear the exploding shells, there was always the faint hope that we may be rescued, or that the Germans would be forced back and the work at this camp discontinued, or perhaps we might soon be sent to another camp where the command-ant was less cruel and inhumane. All of this, of course, was just a case of wishful thinking to help keep our spirits up — drowning men grasping at straws. By the end of the second month, few weeks would pass that did not take one or more of the prisoners with it.

Being a fairly good axe handler, as most Newfoundlanders had to be in those days if they wanted to keep warm, I was put to work chopping down and trimming trees that were being used in the low-lying terrain and swampland to flood the surrounding countryside. One morning, when I returned to the work site, after helping another prisoner carry a tree trunk that was too heavy for him to carry alone, I was surprised to find a guard sitting on one of the logs that I had trimmed up earlier in the morning and still more surprised when, after a careful look all around to make sure that no other guards were nearby, he said in fluent English, "Good morning, comrade, how are you?" He had been a sailor on an English cargo ship for several years before the war, but he was scared stiff, lest he be seen or overheard talking to me.

The reason the *Field Webel* gave the guards for such harsh and inhumane treatment of the prisoners was, he told them, in retaliation for the cruel and brutal treatment that German prisoners were receiving both in England and behind the lines in France. About five or six weeks before our arrival at the camp, he said that all English front-line soldiers had been told by their officers that, because of the shortage of food caused by the sinking of so many merchant ships by German submarines, no more German soldiers were to be taken as prisoners of war, but must instead be shot when captured. Just three weeks before, he told them that four or five hundred of their comrades had been out-flanked and captured by an English division, and after being robbed of all their personal belongings, they were herded into a barbed wire prison cage and machine-gunned to death by their captors.

While this guard and most of the others did not believe that the English would do such an awful thing, there were some who, after listening to so much propaganda, were not so sure. None of them were cruel or brutal like the *Field Webel*, and he [the guard] hoped we would not blame the guards too much for something they could not help and had no control over.

In order to give the guards a rest, we were not compelled to work on Sundays. Every Sunday afternoon, the *Field Webel* would amuse himself and entertain his men by standing just outside our compound, and from a large wicker basket filled with apples (which had been donated by the French fruit growers for the prisoners), he would throw just one apple and wait a few seconds before throwing another. Then he would watch and gloat, as the poor starving prisoners, in their desperate longing and craving for food, wrestled and fought with each other like so many wild animals for possession of the apples. Although it took every last ounce of willpower we possessed, there were still a considerable number of us who had, so far, resisted the temptation to take part in any of those animal-like displays. Some of us, having taken note of the *Field Webel*'s scowl of displeasure toward those of us who took this attitude, decided that we had best stay inside our shack until he got through with his fun.

Then, one Sunday afternoon, our worst fears were suddenly realized. The prisoners who were standing aside, taking no part in the free-for-all, other than that of spectators, were ordered down to the corner of the barbed wire enclosure. The others were told to remain where they were. The *Field Webel* threw an apple to the prisoners in the corner, but no one attempted to pick it up. He threw some more until there were as many apples on the ground as there were prisoners standing in the corner. They were then ordered to pick up the apples, but each of the prisoners held his ground and silently, but firmly, refused to obey.

For a moment or two, the *Field Webel* pondered as though uncertain of his next move. It soon became apparent, however, that he had no intention of permitting a filthy lot of stubborn, English swine to interfere with his pleasure, or to humiliate him in the presence of his men. Ordering several of his guards to fix bayonets and escort him inside the compound, he again ordered the prisoners to pick the apples up, but not one of them made a move to do so. Whether he would have ordered the guards to use their bayonets or not, we will never know.

Before he had time to decide on his next move, the smallest prisoner in the whole camp, nicknamed "the Bantam," stepped directly out in front of him and, in a manner that would have done credit to Hyde Park's best,[13] began making it perfectly clear to this big fat Prussian bully about twice his size just why he and his comrades had refused to pick up the apples. If, he said, the *Field Webel* would agree to offer or present the apples in a humane, civilized manner, both he and his fellow prisoners would be pleased and grateful to accept them, but never would he personally (and he felt the same could be said for his friends) condescend to take part in the animal-like performance demanded by the *Field Webel* for the sole purpose of entertaining himself and his men at the expense of the poor starving prisoners.

By this time, we had all left the barn and shacks to try and find out what all the commotion was about. What we saw was a real heartwarming re-enactment of David and Goliath, but in this case, poor David possessed no weapon — not even a stone — and we were all sorely afraid for his safety. It was both magnificent and horrifying to watch this little Cockney perform, and having fought beside an East London battalion in the Dardanelles, I use the term Cockney with deep and sincere respect. They are unsurpassed in both courage and stamina, which was proven over and over again in the "London Blitz" during the Second World War. What other people do we know who, while their hearts were breaking, could will themselves to laugh and joke with each other while watching their lifelong homes and all of their precious belongings going up in flames?

The *Field Webel* could not restrain himself long enough to hear the Bantam out, but he heard enough to realize and fully understand that here was the kind of hated Englander whose indomitable spirit and fortitude neither he nor any of his so-called super-race would ever be able to conquer or destroy.[14] But now, like the rest of us, he [the Bantam] could fight only in spirit, as we were all well aware that the first sign of physical resistance on his or our part to defend him would be our last, as this huge Prussian monster, who was now being administered the biggest moral defeat of his life, would like nothing better than an excuse to have his guards run us through with their bayonets. Ranting, raving, foaming at the mouth, and snarling like a mad dog, he began with clenched fists to hammer at the lad's mouth and face until he had tired himself out, and our poor friend, the Bantam, whose whole face looked like a piece of newly butchered beef, lay unconscious on the ground.

I remember back in the middle twenties when a couple of German aviators made the first non-stop flight from east to west, across the Atlantic, and again when the author of the book *All Quiet on the Western Front*[15] visited Christie Street Hospital, where I was a patient at the time. Some of the staff there, as well as many letters to the press, objected to so much ex-enemy hero worship and fuss being made over them when so many of our own Canadian boys had been so badly treated as prisoners of war in Germany. But some other people, whose only contact with the war was in the huge profits they made from it, called POW mistreatment fiction. Even two of Toronto's leading newspapers carried editorials that definitely stated all the stories of starvation and ill treatment brought back by some German-hating prisoners of war were false. Too bad those newspaper editors and war profiteers could not have been given just one glimpse of what my fellow prisoners and I were seeing there in that awful compound on a beautiful 1917 November afternoon.

Not that I had any objection to the visit of the author and flyers — in fact, I was pleased to see them. After all, they were not responsible for the war any more than our own soldiers were. Besides, the war had been over for ten years at the time of their visit. They had both earned and deserved our goodwill — especially so the author of *All Quiet*, whose book was so precisely accurate as to what life was really like, both in and out of the trenches, that the author could well be writing about a group of young soldiers on our side of no man's land, rather than on his own. But surely there was no reason or need for those Toronto editors and their profiteer friends to accuse the returned war prisoners of lying so that (as one or more of them later admitted and apologized for) the two visiting German celebrities would feel more at ease and welcome.

Although the Bantam got well enough to work again, he never did fully recover from the terrible beating he took, and a few weeks later, he died, but as one or more of our number were dying every week about this time, we could not be sure whether or not the cruel beating was the sole cause of his death. Some of his friends dug and prepared his grave on a Saturday evening beside the graves of other prisoners who had also died of ill treatment, including malnutrition and starvation, but waited until early Sunday morning when the *Field Webel* would not be around to interfere as some of us gathered to say goodbye.

None of us possessed a Bible or a prayer book any more, but I could remember much of the burial ritual from having heard my father repeat it so many times at the gravesides of our friends and neighbours in the little village outport where I was born. My father was neither a priest nor a minister, but frequently, owing to weather conditions and the difficulty of travel during winter, substituted for both. So after repeating as much of it as I could recall and attempting a few appropriate words about him and his beloved bow-bells,[16] which he so often tried to explain and define to the overseas boys (the ANZACs) when they teased or bantered him re the definition of a Cockney, we said a sad farewell to one of England's little men who died with dignity and courage, equal to any of her greatest.

Following the death of the Bantam, the Sunday afternoon apple matinees were discontinued, and except for his daily inspection of the work under construction, we saw very little of the *Field Webel* anymore, but even that was much too much. Most of the guards (not all) would warn us if and when they saw him coming, by shouting their orders a little louder and in a more unfriendly tone, but as soon as he was gone, they would relax and permit us to slow down. Frequently, when a prisoner became too weak or sick to fill his quota of work, one or more of the guards would pitch in and help the rest of us make it up while he rested behind a hedge or brush pile, hidden in case the *Field Webel* should make unexpected appearance.

In the small village outport on the northeast coast of Newfoundland where I was born in 1895, there were no doctors, hospitals, or medical care of any kind, and those of us unfortunate enough to get sick from something a dose of cod liver oil or a cup of juniper tea could not cure were nailed up in little pine boxes and taken to the community churchyard. Consequently, none but the fittest survived, and except for wounds, yellow jaundice, and dysentery contracted while serving in the Dardanelles, I had never been sick a day in my life. Having worked in a sawmill ten hours per day, six days per week, from the time I was twelve years old until I enlisted at eighteen years of age, hard work and hardship had always been my lot, which, although I hate to think so, could probably have accounted for my being in much better physical condition at the end of three months at that horrible slave labour camp than were most of the other prisoners.

While my fellow prisoners, most of whom were from the British Isles, were attending good schools and taking part in their various games and sports, which should have been the right, not just a privilege, of every boy and girl everywhere, I had the misfortune of having been born in Newfoundland. I was compelled to work a full sixty hours each and every week, fifty-two weeks a year, carrying heavy water-soaked lumber from the mill-saws to the drying yard, two hundred feet away.

Is it any wonder that the Prussian general who interrogated me at Ghent was amazed when I informed him that none of the men in my regiment had been conscripted by the English government, as he had supposed, but were all volunteers and had enlisted of their own free will? "Good God," he replied, "what has England ever done for your poverty-stricken island and its people to merit such loyalty?" To that question I had no answer. Maybe there was one, but I didn't have it.

# CHAPTER SEVEN

## PRISONER OF WAR, OCTOBER 1917

The "slave camp" environment Manuel describes was not fully understood by the Allied military leadership or general public until after the war's end. It is a phenomenon that has attracted little serious scholarly attention. This fact may be attributable to the far greater scrutiny directed to later Second World War horrors associated with Nazi Germany's concentration camps, "final solution" Jewish extermination plans, Stalin-inspired Ukrainian genocides, and similar, better-documented atrocities.

However, what Manuel recounts is both powerful and highly instructive. The "slave camp" is a chilling precursor for what lay ahead in the Second World War. His escape attempt, with its black comedy aspects, and his recapture are defining points in the entire Manuel narrative. The escape took place in March 1918. It arguably provides the most detailed first-hand account of POW life and attempted escape by a North American Great War soldier ever published.

———

The probabilities for a successful escape from that horrible slave camp had been discussed, pro and con, almost endlessly, ever since our arrival there in early October, but in our weakened condition and without food to take along, the chances of making it all the way to the Allied lines would probably be less than one in ten. Despite the odds, four of us, now firmly convinced that we would never be permitted to leave in any other way, were seriously thinking of attempting to try it. There was little doubt that the Germans, having held this sector of the front for such a long time, would have the many lines of defence well fortified and closely watched.

However, as the guards no longer took the precaution of checking our number when we quit work for camp each evening, like they had done during the first two months, this could give us an excellent opportunity to step behind a hedge at quitting time, and with a little luck, [we] might not be missed until the lineup for work the next morning. We would then be permitted a full night of travel before the troops in that vicinity could be alerted.

From the sound of the heavy artillery that we could sometimes hear when the wind was in a certain direction, we estimated the distance to be thirty-five to forty miles, but as we dared not travel during the daytime and only with extreme caution at night, it would take at least three and maybe as many as five nights to sneak through and around the many and varied types of gun batteries and other defence fortifications. The four of us who had now definitely made up our minds about going fully realized that we could not again endure such a long journey without food, as we had done on the train trip from Dendermonde, and as it was now winter, there would be little or nothing that we could salvage from the deserted French farms.

Our only hope of success (or even survival) would be in saving at least half of our daily allowance of bread during the next two to three weeks. Our first attempt to carry this plan through was a dismal failure. Having once tasted the bread, two of our number were unable to resist the temptation of consuming the whole issue. We solved or overcame that problem by pledging to do without and put aside our full portion every other morning.

Only people who have at some time been for months on the verge of starvation can fully appreciate the nigh-to-superhuman willpower required in keeping such a pledge. This was not at all like a civilian jailbreak one reads or hears about over the radio. Once inside our shack, away from the guards, we could discuss and formulate our plan freely. There were no eavesdroppers or so-called stool pigeons to worry about, and I doubt if most of the guards, who by this time were almost as sorry for us as we were for ourselves, would have informed on us if they had known.

Although most of us tended to think the French occupied the trenches on that particular sector of the front, we were not at all certain, but dared not ask the guards lest they became suspicious as to what we were up to. We later learned that the *Field Webel* had planted several spies among the guards, who not only spied on the prisoners but on their own comrades as well, so as it turned out, we had been wise in not asking any questions about the front. If it were the French and if, by some miracle, we were fortunate enough to make it all the way to their front lines, we would still have their sentries to contend with before we were out of the woods. And I had often heard it said that those French boys were more or less trigger-happy, and where the least bit of doubt existed, they were inclined to shoot first and ask questions after.

One of the prisoners could speak French fluently, and although he was not coming with us, claiming the trip would be just too much for him (nor could he ever find the willpower to save any of his bread), [he] agreed to teach us what he could. He had us rehearse, over and over again for a week or more, the answers to questions that he thought we would most likely be challenged with by the French sentries, when and if we reached their front lines.

The big drawback with this was the probability of a special pass or recognition word or words known only to the French themselves. If, however, we could manage to conceal ourselves close enough to their firing line to make our appearance in daylight, they would readily see at a glance that we were either escaped prisoners of war or ghosts, in which case there would be no need to challenge us at all. In the meantime, we would just have to wait and cross that bridge when we came to it.

The guards did not bother to keep a very close watch when we took time out to obey the calls of nature, which gave us time to hide the bread we were saving for the trip, high on a ledge, underneath an old stone bridge, which we covered with pieces of wood and stone to protect it from the birds and other small animals. The German wartime bread, consisting of so many synthetics, would keep indefinitely, if kept reasonably dry.

On the evening preceding our departure, the other two boys who had planned on going with Brown[1] and me informed us that they had weakened and eaten their share of the bread. Poor devils — with such a terrible yearning and craving for food, they deserved much credit in having resisted the temptation to eat our share of the bread as well as their own. They were so despondent and regretful, begging and pleading with us to accept their issue of bread the following morning, and so too did four other prisoners. This we refused to do. All of the other prisoners were rooting for us, which, of course, they should have been, because the very first thing we planned on doing if we were lucky enough to make it to England was to make a full report to the British branch of the International Red Cross organization. We hoped they would get in touch with the Red Cross people of neutral Switzerland, Denmark, Holland, or Norway regarding the awful conditions that existed at our slave camp.

Brown and I did as little work as we could get away with that day, and the other boys helped as much as they could to cover for us. We had said our farewells the night before. One of Brown's Australian buddies insisted on giving him his lucky piece — a little gold statuette of Saint Christopher, supposed to take care of travellers on a long and perilous journey. Another lad I did not even know talked me into accepting his lucky rabbit's foot, and while most of us regard the wearing of such charms and tokens as nothing more or less than pure superstition, to the people who believe in such things, they are just as real and comforting as the many faiths and religious beliefs are to others, and we felt that both prisoners made a considerable sacrifice in parting with their treasured symbols.

When quitting time came, we experienced no difficulty in hiding behind some willow brush until the prisoners and their guards were out of sight, and after recovering our cache of bread, [we] moved far enough back in the undergrowth to be safe from view, in case our absence was discovered by the guards on their way back to camp. We waited there, about thirty minutes, for deep twilight and then began our long and perilous journey in the direction of the enemy's front-line trenches. We could hear the noise of trucks and horse-drawn vehicles on the road, far over to our right, all through the night. We passed by several farm buildings, all of which were deserted but appeared to be undamaged, leading us to surmise that the French army must have voluntarily retreated from this territory early in the war, in preference for a better-suited defence terrain farther back.

We came upon the first shell hole just before daybreak, and judging from the thick growth of grass and weeds inside the lip, it had probably been made two or more years before. Afraid of being seen, we half circled what appeared to be a small deserted hamlet, but despite all the precaution, we must have covered well over a third of the way during our first long night and felt rather disappointed at not being within hearing distance of the quick-firing guns when daylight came. There was no doubt whatever about our being headed in the right direction as we could distinctly hear the occasional long-distance shellfire away over on our right front and see the reflections of the exploding shells in the skyline.

At the first sign of dawn, we decided to hole up for the day. We selected a wooded lot with plenty of undergrowth within five hundred feet of an old stone farmhouse and close enough to the highway to see the traffic coming and going. While one of us slept, or tried to sleep, the other kept a very close watch. The highway was more or less busy all day, but no one entered or left the old farmhouse. We were both very cold, and although we had a few matches stolen for us by one of the prisoners who helped out in the swill kitchen, we dared not build a fire, lest it be seen from the highway. So far, we had resisted the craving urge to eat some of our bread, agreeing to hold off until we were ready to leave at night, when the need for it would be much greater.

Early in the afternoon, after watching the old farmhouse all morning and being almost certain it was unoccupied, we decided to go over and take a look around. The fairly thick growth of bushes and the tall dead grass served to provide us with ample cover on the way. After cautiously peeping through all the windows at the back, none of which were broken, we entered a side door by pulling a string that lifted an old pioneer-type wood latch. The first room we saw was strewn with very old, but fairly clean, straw. The other rooms and all of the upstairs were completely bare, but the back-room kitchen, which was about as big as the other three rooms combined, contained an old worn couch, a rough-sawn plank table, some long wooden benches, and a very old-fashioned large-size wood- or coal-burning stove.

Much to our surprise, pleasure, joy (and all the superlatives that it would be possible to add), when we drained the liquid from a small barrel-size keg that was half hidden behind one of the benches, we found six large pickled herrings of a kind I had often seen the guards eating for lunch, back at the work site. There was also an old, rusty, unopened can, about one-half gallon in size, which must have taken us the better part of an hour to pound open with a rock.

The exhilarating thrill of delight experienced by some old sourdough prospector, who, after searching the wilderness for years in vain and then accidentally discovering what is known as the "motherlode" on his way home, would just be a mild sensation compared to what Brown and I felt on discovering that this rusty old can was filled with delicious (and, to Brown and me, precious) blood sausage, frequently called blood pudding. Just then, we would not have traded those six herrings or that tin of congealed blood for all the gold and diamonds ever mined. A pair of well-worn military jackboots, which must have belonged to a giant-sized trooper (the kind worn by German soldiers), stood in a corner by the couch. They were several sizes too big for either Brown or me and we both needed shoes, but not half as much as we needed food.

There were no signs of recent occupation, and we concluded that the sausage and herring had either been forgotten or purposely left behind, perhaps a couple of years or more before, when they had more of this kind of food than they cared for. With all of this extra, unexpected food, there was no purpose in waiting until night to break our fast, as we had previously planned on doing. So we each ate a piece of our bread, two whole herrings (including the heads, fins, and guts), and a very small portion of the blood sausage. While that would have been as much or more than I could eat in two meals now, at that time, my desperate craving for food was such that I could have eaten twice as much without having appeased my hunger.

After reassuring ourselves that no German soldiers were in the vicinity, we did not think it necessary to keep further watch, so we lay down close together, covering ourselves with straw for warmth, and fell fast asleep. It was near dark when we awakened, famished with thirst brought on by eating the very salty herring. We found an old well near the barn. The water looked rather dirty, but we drank it anyway, although I did not drink half as much as Brown and cautioned him against drinking too much of it as well.

As soon as it grew dark enough, we wrapped the two remaining herrings and the tin of blood sausage in a piece of dirty old burlap and took off into the unknown for a second night. We could still hear the traffic on the highway nearby, but no lights were now being shown that we could see. About two hours before dawn, we came dangerously close to stumbling over the base of a huge, long-range cannon, concealed and well camouflaged behind a stand of low-lying trees. We did not linger to find out whether it was manned or not, but hurriedly circled back and around to the left. From here on, we would have to proceed much more cautiously, as the sounds of whiz-bangs and other types of fast-firing guns had now become very distinct, and once that morning, I thought I heard machine-gun fire.

We must have passed between several long-range cannons in the twelve or more miles that we made during the night, as some were being fired from behind us the next day. A couple of heavy French or British shells exploded about three or four miles on our right front, near the highway, next day, which, in all probability, was the target sought.

We had come to a small running brook, where we would have plenty of good drinking water for the following day, so we stopped a couple of hours earlier than we would otherwise have done. When day did come, we were not so sure we had chosen wisely, as we were within just a few hundred feet of several high-calibre guns. Owing to the low-lying terrain, the highway was hidden from view, but a side or crossroad, directly in front of us, was busy all day.

Occasionally, the men taking supplies to the guns would pass by our hideout, close enough for us to overhear them talking. Their firing line could not be more than another seven or eight miles from here, but whether we could make it all the way in one more night would depend on the number of obstacles we would have to contend with along the way. We had already crossed one of their support (reserve) trenches without incident. There was sure to be at least one more (maybe two) before we reached their firing line.

With plenty of water close by to take care of our thirst, we ate the last two herrings early that morning. At night, we each had a piece of bread and a little more of the blood sausage, leaving us with eight pieces of bread and more than half of the blood sausage for the next twenty-four or forty-eight hours, which was four times the amount and much better food than we would have received back at the slave camp. It turned out to be a nice sunny winter day, and sheltered as we were from the wind, we were fairly warm and comfortable, much more so than on the previous day, and finding more to talk about, the time seemed to pass much faster. We could see the soldiers coming and going a full minute or so before they passed our underbrush hideout, allowing us ample time to conceal ourselves before they passed by.

Brown was thirty-three years of age, which seemed to me at the time, being only twenty-one, to be well into middle age. He was about six feet tall, and when I first saw him at the slave camp, he was a very good-looking man, but now, like the rest of us, he was just a heap of bones with a very loose skin covering — the flesh having long since disappeared. While all starving, skeleton-like men are displeasing to the eye, the taller man, perhaps because of his longer-shaped head, appears to have a more repulsive ghostlike appearance than a shorter man. He was fairly well educated and had visited many parts of the world, including Canada. His family had migrated to Australia from Yorkshire, England, when he was ten years old. His people were sheep ranchers, and as the whole family had already made two trips back to England and the continent on holidays, I gathered they must have done very well financially. He was very modest, however, and not inclined to boast, which probably is why I liked him so well.

We started out a little early that night and must have covered close to half of the remaining distance to the front line before midnight. Every now and then, we could see flashes and feel the recoil of the nearby guns. We had been trying to find some kind of bottle or can suitable to carry water in ever since leaving camp, but being unable to locate one, we were obliged to hunt for hideouts where water could be obtained. Tonight though, after searching as much and as long as we dared in vain, we would just have to do without. Several times during the night, we came close enough to some of the guns to overhear the crews talking to each other. I had picked up a little of the language over the months, but not enough to fool any German, and there would be no sense in my attempting to do so. Our one and only chance of success lay in keeping out of sight.

Although there was very little shooting from either side, some rifle or machine-gun fire could be heard far over on our left front. We passed within yards of whiz-bangs and other types of quick-firing artillery pieces, before holing up for the last day. Even though we moved at only a snail's pace during the last half of the night, we were not more than two to three miles from the German front trench when day broke. About one hour before taking cover for the last day, we came within inches of being caught, after being compelled to sneak between two or more batteries of guns that were so close together we could hear one of the crew snoring as we crept through.

When daylight came, we could see guns and soldiers almost everywhere, but so far, it was the quietest front I had ever seen. Scarcely a shot was being fired from either side, and it appeared as though both sides had sat down to wait each other out. Whether this was just the calm before the storm, we had no way of knowing.

This, our third and last day (and fourth, and last, night), developed into one of the most miserable, nerve-wracking twenty-four hours that I have ever experienced. The very small shell hole that we had picked in the dark was much too shallow to protect or hide us from view. Some German soldiers passed by so close I could have reached out my hand and touched them. All through the first half of the day, we were compelled to lie flat on our stomachs, with our faces close to the bottom of the shell hole, holding our breath and expecting to hear the fatal words every time a soldier went by. But for the fact that our dirty, tattered old khaki-coloured uniforms blended so well with the surroundings, providing us with nigh-to-perfect camouflage, we would have been discovered and recaptured within an hour.

Just after dark, as we were about to leave, poor Brown became ill, seized with what appeared to be stomach cramps, which caused him to moan so loud, I felt sure the Germans would hear him. I had cautioned him against drinking so much of what could have been polluted water, after eating the very salty herring, back at the old farmhouse. He was much too ill to continue the journey and pleaded with me to go on alone, promising not [to] give himself up until sufficient time had elapsed for my reaching the Allied lines. Poor Brown — he was as much concerned for my safety as for his own, but I would not have gone and left him there sick and helpless for all the freedom in the world, nor would he have gone and left me. Several times, I was on the verge of giving myself up and appealing for help, but he kept begging me not to, saying that if I did and he got better, he would not be able to live with himself after.

As soon as it grew dark enough to hide us, we moved to a much better location, out of sight and sound of the soldiers. I massaged his stomach and got him to throw up by pushing my fingers down his throat. After considerable persuasion, I got him to eat a little bread, thinking perhaps it might help to counteract the effects of the polluted water. At first he rebelled, claiming he was much too sick to get it down, but when I told him he could either eat the bread or have me give myself up and seek help, he gave in and promised to do whatever I thought best. I broke off small bits of bread and fed him slowly, whispering a prayer with every piece. Within an hour or so, he was feeling much better, and needless to say, so was I.

We were both very thirsty. There was no water to be had, however, and I was secretly hoping that we would not find any for at least three or four hours, as I felt sure now that so much bad water, plus the briny salt herring, had been the cause for his cramps. Starving men, trying to appease their desperate yearning and craving for food, are inclined to drink much more water than is good for them. It had been dark now for two hours or longer, and Brown was anxious to get going, but he still looked like a very sick man, and although he kept trying to reassure me, I knew he was still suffering considerable pain, so I insisted that we wait an hour or two longer. Being already so near the front line, there would be ample time to make it the remainder of the way, even if we waited until midnight.

I persuaded Brown to eat a little more bread and as much of the blood sausage as his stomach would take, as we would either be in the Allied lines or recaptured by the Germans before another sunrise. There was little purpose in not appeasing our hunger as much as possible. I did, however, save a few pieces of bread, in case the cramps recurred again. Both deeply conscious that, after tonight, we might never meet or see each other again, we shook hands and wished each other luck in case we might not have another opportunity to do so after leaving our hideout. Having suffered so much from hunger, cold, and brutality during the past five months, neither of us were experiencing quite as much fear as we would have under normal conditions, but to say that we were unafraid would be downright false — anyone with as much will and desire to live as we had must have [had] some fear of dying, although Brown showed not the slightest signs of any.

We wormed our way forward, very slowly and with extreme care. We could hear men talking much of the time, but the voices seemed to be coming from below the surface of the ground. Except for the occasional bursts of machine-gun fire, away over on our left flank, the war could well be over, and if the Allies opposite this sector of the front possessed such deep and well-constructed trenches as those we saw during the next seven or eight hours, both sides could be saving themselves much work and money and inflicting every bit as much damage on each other [as] if they never fired a shot. Those German soldiers were just about as safe in those deep shell-proof dugouts as they would have been back home in bed.

We soon discovered that the voices we kept hearing were coming from a deep communication trench leading directly into their front-line trench. The ridges of soil thrown up at the side gave us some protection and also served as a guide to the firing line. Now and again, we could see the muzzles of many rifles and sometimes see the coal-scuttle-type, steel helmets of the taller men protruding about the top as they marched in single file, back through the trench, toward the rear.

Without watches, we could only guess at the time, but we reached the front line hours before dawn. "What a front line," I once heard some English officers bragging about how much better the British trenches were than the French trenches. Maybe they were, as I never saw a French trench, but they should have seen how much better the German trenches were than the British trenches — particularly so, the steel-and-concrete machine-gun nests and the thirty- and forty-feet-deep shell-proof chain of dugouts that extended most of the way from Switzerland to the North Sea.

The Germans must have been here for years in order to have such a magnificent defence system; except for the firing step, the front trench was much deeper than a British trench. But its real value and protection lay in the countless deep, slanted bays and traverses, curving in and out, similar to the teeth in a giant pit saw. I doubt very much if a direct hit from one of our most powerful guns would have caused enough damage to pay for the shell.

Keeping ourselves well hidden at the back of the trench, we could distinctly see the outline of three sentries, spaced about seventy or more feet apart, but because of the many bays and curves in the trench for protection against crossfire, the sentry on the right and the one on the left were in a more advanced position than the sentry in the centre. All three appeared to be very much alert and keeping a very sharp watch in the direction of the Allied lines. The very night that we hoped it would be dark, wet, and gloomy, to aid us over the firing trench and out across no man's land, turned out to be the brightest and least suited for the purpose. Nothing short of a miracle could prevent our being seen by one or all of those sentries if we attempted to cross here. Machine guns, most of which appeared to be unmanned but otherwise ready for action, were mounted all along the line. The crews for those guns would be sleeping, or resting, safe and comfortable in their shell-proof dugouts beneath the trench, from where they could reach their guns in seconds, if alerted or attacked.

The trench was far too wide to jump across, had we dared to do so, and in order to get over, we would have to slide down the back and then climb out over the parapet at the front. Unless the sentries became much less vigilant, such a manoeuvre would not be possible at this location, and as they showed no signs of doing so during the hour or more that we waited there, we decided to try another section of the line, where we could perhaps find a weak spot on one of the traverses or bays where the sentries were not so vigilant. Withdrawing for about a quarter of a mile the way we had come, we turned right for about half a mile, with a second right turn taking us back to a different sector of the firing line. The situation here was identical with the one we had just left, and after taking a quick look all around, we repeated the same kind of manoeuvre for a third and finally a fourth time.

On our fourth and last trip, we came to a second communication trench, leading into the firing line. It was fairly deep, but not very wide, and on making sure it was empty, [we] crossed without incident. Another mile or so brought us to a third trench, where we again turned right and back to the front trench. Except for those well-trained, wide-awake sentries, we could have gone almost anywhere on the surface at will. We never saw another German with his head above ground after leaving our hideout, back near the support trench, several hours before. The whole picture, here at our fourth and last stop, appeared to be precisely the same as the other three, and that is exactly what it was — a complete duplication. The German technicians, with their passion for detail and thoroughness, had most likely measured the distance between each sentry and gun with a tape line.

The nearest sentry at this last location appeared to be a little more nervous or restless than any of the others. Every minute or so, he would sit down on what could have been a box or a large block of wood. His head was always above the parapet, however, and he seemed to have his mind on his work, keeping a sharp watch in the direction of no man's land. Oh, how we wished that the French, or whoever was occupying the trenches over there, would open fire and cause enough excitement to distract those sentries long enough to get us out, over the parapet, and beyond their barbed wire, into no man's land. Once I heard Brown whisper, "Oh, what I wouldn't give for one of London's pea soup fogs."

With little or no hope of making a successful crossing at this location and too close to daybreak to hunt further, I suggested to Brown that we withdraw a mile or so and locate a suitable shell hole and sweat it out for another day, permitting us more time and perhaps a more suitable night to try again. Ever since leaving camp, Brown [had] insisted on my taking the initiative in making all of the decisions, contending that I possessed a much keener sense of direction and danger than he did. This was definitely not so — his ideas and sense of direction [were] every bit as good and perhaps even better.

I had tried my best to convince him of this on our first night out by telling him of an incident back home in Newfoundland where I had once got lost in the woods and was compelled to spend the whole night less than ten miles from where I was born and lived. "Getting lost in the woods," he replied, "could happen to the best of foresters." Brown knew ranchers where he lived in Australia who got themselves lost while just visiting their neighbours. He forgot to mention that the majority of Australian sheep ranchers and their neighbours lived anywhere from twenty to one hundred or more miles apart. Now, when he showed signs of hesitation in agreeing to my suggestion, I suddenly realized that he had taken about as much as he could endure and concluded that it must be tonight or never.

We must have spent the better part of an hour taking stock and looking the place over before deciding to take the final plunge. We managed to ease ourselves down the back of the trench and out over the parapet without making a sound; flat on our stomachs, with bated breath, we hugged the ground. Never before had I seen so few shell holes around a front-line trench. There was not a single shell hole within twenty yards or more of the trench that was wide and deep enough to take cover in.

[After] touching Brown on the arm as a signal, we wormed our way forward for another ten or twelve feet, toward the Allied lines. So near and yet so far. We were within three or four hundred yards of friends and freedom when I was to hear again, for the second time in less than eight months, that one dreaded, threatening word — "Halt."

# CHAPTER EIGHT

## BAVARIA, JANUARY 1918

In the German trenches, Manuel is interrogated once more by a high-ranking German officer. During the course of interrogation, Manuel tells this officer about the slave camp conditions. The Germans are disgusted with his description and they take particular care to ensure Manuel and Brown are well fed. Both soldiers are attended to by doctors, and Brown is rushed to hospital for surgery to deal with his appendicitis.

———

When we had satisfied the lieutenant that there were only two of us, he ordered the men back to their rest quarters, [and] said a few complimentary words to the sentry who had been responsible for our recapture. He gave Brown a kind of reassuring touch on the shoulder and signalled us to walk ahead of him down through the trench. We turned at the first communication trench, and after following it for about a half mile or less, descended about twenty-five or thirty steps into a very deep dugout that had all the appearances of a home away from home — in fact, it was much better furnished than any home I ever lived in.

The walls contained several large maps, a full-size painting of the kaiser, and the photographs of two beautiful women. The floor was covered with a large mat or carpet. There was a rather long, nicely polished table and a dozen or more chairs. A corporal sat at a combination desk and work table, taking care of a telegraph set and two or three telephones. The whole place was illuminated with electrical lights. The corporal got up and saluted the lieutenant as we entered. I gathered, from what I could understand of the conversation, that the lieutenant was telling the corporal to inform the commanding officer about the two prisoners and to find out what he was to do with us. The corporal went to the far end of the room, drew back a curtain, and walked through to what, in all probability, was the commander's sleeping quarters. He reappeared almost immediately and asked the lieutenant to wait a few minutes.

It was not long before the curtain again parted and a rather tall, good-looking officer came out. I think he was a colonel, but I had not seen enough of them to be sure of their rank. I knew, however (or rather, I thought I knew from his haughty-appearing manner), that he was another of those arrogant and domineering Prussians similar to the tyrant who had given me such a hard time when he quizzed me for information back at Ghent.

We all stood up, [and] the two Germans saluted; Brown and I had already removed our old bonnets, so we just stood at attention until he told us to sit down. He talked for a minute or two with the lieutenant, then turned to us and said in broken, but easily understood, English, "So, you are the two boys responsible for so much disturbance. Don't you think I should have you both shot for waking our men from their sleep and causing us so much trouble?" He appeared to be waiting for an answer, so I told him he could do nothing worse to us than what had not already been done unless he did have us shot, and considering what we had been through, I doubted if being shot would be much ... worse.

I waited for that blast of Prussian wrath and arrogance, which I felt was bound to come, but was very much surprised when he told me to keep talking. I told him of the *Field Webel's* cruel and inhumane treatment of the prisoners and of how we were compelled to work from dawn to dark on an eighth of a loaf of black synthetic bread and a pint of *mangelwurzel* swill. When I told him about the apple episode and of the terrible beating our friend the Bantam had taken, he stopped me long enough to translate part of what I had said to the lieutenant, the gist of which I understood. "This poor damn Englander is telling the truth and that bitch's son should be shot." The lieutenant, who I had already sensed felt sorry for us, replied, "Ya, ya, so, so."

The commander said he was surprised that we had made it all the way to no man's land in our starved and weakened condition, and if we were his men, he would be proud of us, but war was hell and we were just another two of its victims. He was sorry for our hard luck in not making it all the way through, but pleased that his own men were alert and keeping such a sharp watch up at the front line. We would be sent back to divisional headquarters in the afternoon, and while he would not likely be consulted about our punishment for attempting to escape, he felt sure that it would not be as bad as our treatment at the camp had been. The commander told us he would see to it that the proper authorities were informed of our inhumane prison camp treatment. He then ordered the lieutenant to make sure we were given a good meal and as much as we could eat before being sent back to divisional headquarters.

My first impression of this proud, haughty-looking Prussian officer had been completely wrong, and though our disappointment and despair at being recaptured was nigh to overwhelming, it might have been (although I have no positive proof) the best possible thing that could have happened — not for Brown and me, but for our friends and comrades back at the slave camp. I am as sure as anyone can be without actual proof that it was this front-line Prussian officer we had to thank for the many improvements that took place shortly after, including twice the amount of food and finally the transfer of all the surviving prisoners to registered POW camps and hospitals back in Germany.

The commander dismissed us by saying something along the lines of "better luck next time" and then went back to his room. The lieutenant phoned for an escort, and while we waited, he tried to tell us in German about his good, kind commander, and I sensed by the way his face lit up he was not saying it just to make Brown and me feel better, but really meant what he said. When the two soldiers came to take us farther back to the rear, he handed one of them a note for the mess sergeant, gave us both a friendly wave (which in all probability was as close, or even closer, to a handshake as the rules permitted), wished us the equivalent of "God be with you" in German, then headed back to his post, in the front-line trench.

I have often pondered as to why soldiers, including combatant officers on both sides of no man's land, tend to be more considerate and friendly in and around the front-line trenches than many of them do elsewhere. Is it because of the constant nearness to death? If so, it would be a brilliant idea and make for a much better world if each and every one of us would contemplate on being in the front line every day of our lives.

Together with the two guards, one in front and the other at the back, we marched in single file, back through the narrow communication trench. Poor Brown was becoming more tired and weak with every step, and just before we reached the end of the trench, he collapsed. One of the guards ran on ahead and sent two other men back with a stretcher. I followed them down into another of those huge, deep dugouts, where a platoon or more of troops were just sitting down to breakfast. A Red Cross corporal fixed a place for Brown to lie down. He felt his pulse, took his temperature, gave him a drink of water, and then disappeared through one of the narrow openings that I found [out] later led to a whole chain of dugouts.

While I sat there talking to Brown, trying to cheer him up as best I could, the corporal returned with a very young doctor who, when he had examined Brown, said to me in German that my comrade was sick. He told the corporal not to give Brown anything to eat and then left. A few minutes later, another first-aid man came and beckoned me to follow him, and after walking through several dugouts, we came to one that was being used as a first-aid or casualty clearing station. The young doctor, who was now talking on the telephone, held up his finger for me to come over. He handed me the receiver, and the same voice, in broken English, that I had heard earlier in the morning said, "Englander, none of our men there can speak English and the doctor tells me that your friend is very sick and will die if not operated on today, so he is going to the hospital right away."

When I asked him why Brown must be operated on, he replied that he had forgotten the English word for it, but it was something that stores in the guts and sometimes blows up and the doctor thinks it may blow up today. I guessed it might be appendicitis and repeated the word. "Ya, ya, yes, yes, that is the word. Now you tell your friend what his trouble is. He will get well again soon. Sorry, you cannot go with him. You must wait there." I thanked him, and he said "Ya, ya, good luck Englander," and hung up. In the meantime, they had brought Brown through from the other dugout, where the doctor had given him some kind of drug and he appeared to be feeling much better. I told him what the commander had said over the phone, and somehow, we both managed to keep a stiff upper lip (as the English call it) when we said goodbye, but each knew well enough what the other was feeling.

For some reason, I was not sent back to divisional headquarters until the following afternoon. The few soldiers left at the dugout during the day, including the doctor and his Red Cross men, were very kind and sympathetic, offering me all the food I could eat, which, if Brown had still been with me, would have compensated some for the disappointments and heartbreaks of the past four days, but now it helped only to make my eyes water and the big lump that was already in my throat just that much bigger.

The doctor gave me a complete checkup. I think he was trying to find a reason, other than loss of weight, which would not have been accepted, for sending me to rejoin Brown at the hospital, but apparently, I was still much too tough and endurable. The first-aid boys permitted me to take a nice, warm bath under their shower. They also gave me a worn, but clean, flannel shirt and a pair of underpants to replace the dirty old rags I was wearing. Late in the afternoon next day, a couple of soldiers walked me back about four miles to one of their ammunition dumps, where some trucks were being unloaded, and later in the evening, when the trucks returned with another load, I was sent back with one of the drivers. I was given a good meal and had a nice warm cot to sleep on that night, but the following morning, I was paraded before another of those Englander-haters, who, after making some nasty remarks about prison being much too good for English swine, sentenced me to twenty-eight days of solitary confinement.

The jail cell was about six feet wide and eight feet long. The small iron-barred window, up near the ceiling, was way over my head and closed to within an inch of being shut. When I asked the guard if he would open it up a bit, he said he had been ordered not to, or German words to that effect. The only glimpse I ever got of the outside was when the guard opened the door twice each day to pass my food through. A piece of heavyweight tarpaulin spread over some straw on the stone floor served as a bed, but most of the nights were so cold [that] I wrapped the canvas around me and paced the few short steps back and forth in the cell to keep from freezing, sleeping as much as I could when the sun had warmed the place up a little during the day. I was given a fifth of bread each morning and a bowl of fairly thick soup at night, which was much better tasting and far more nourishing than the swill back at the slave camp, but still not enough to prevent my yearning for more. I never saw or spoke to another person, except the guard, who was not inclined to be friendly during the entire twenty-eight days.

When I was in the hospital at Ghent, one of the nursing orderlies, admiring my watch, asked if he could buy it, and because he had been so good to me, I lacked the courage to say no, so in exchange for two of Charles Dickens's books, printed in English, which he managed to find in some downtown bookstore, plus thirty German marks, I let him have the watch, and while the books had long since been worn out or used up for various purposes by the boys at the slave camp, I still possessed the thirty marks, which, at that time, was worth about seven or eight dollars. I offered my jailer the thirty marks if he would bring me some English reading. Although he kept the thirty marks, all he ever brought back was a cheap, worn German Bible, which he likely borrowed or stole from one of his comrades.

Even if I could have read German, it would have helped very little. The Bible, being one of the very few books my father could ever afford, had been read and reread so often by both of us and was so much a part of my very brief and meager education that I could — and still can — quote much of it from memory. Strange how some of those German soldiers could be so mean and miserable, while most of them, if permitted, were kind and considerate. Of course, this applies to most other nationalities as much as to the Germans. I recall an incident in France the year before that was equally as cruel and brutal as anything I saw the Germans do, with the exception of the *Field Webel*'s brutality.

Another company signaller and I were sent to one of the training classes in Rouen for a week's instruction course on a new type of telegraph set that had just been introduced to the army. On our second day there, we saw some German prisoners being marched over from their prison camp across the street, and because a few of them were apparently not moving fast enough to please their French guards, the guards were shouting a whole lot of vile and dirty French phrases and kept pricking the poor

German prisoners in their backsides with the tips of their bayonets. Some British soldiers, including most of those from overseas, became angry and indignant, shouting at the guards to stop. The French officer in charge resented our interference, informing us that they were fighting a war, not operating a nursery, and if we were such good *Boche*[1] lovers and did not like the way his men were treating our friends, we could move the hell out of there and mind our own damn business.

Except for the long days and nights of monotony and loneliness, I was holding up physically much better in this jail than I would have done back at the slave camp. Having no work to do, plus the little extra and much better food, I doubt if I lost any more weight during the whole twenty-eight days. It would not have been possible to lose much more, as I could feel little or no flesh between the skin and bones on any part of my body.

On being released from solitary, I was sent back to the slave camp. Many changes had taken place during my absence, and all of them, I am happy to say, for the better. The bread ration had not yet been increased any, but the swill was now 100 percent better, and each prisoner was given about twice as much of it, which was still not enough to keep body and soul together. The prisoners had been told that their bread rations would be doubled as soon as arrangements could be made with the quarter-master. They made good on that promise a couple of weeks later, but by then, I was no longer there.

An epidemic of typhus had broken out while I was away, and doctors had been sent in to inoculate and vaccinate everyone at the camp, which was, of course, more for the protection of their own men rather than for the welfare of the prisoners. All of the surviving prisoners were moved to one shack, while the other one was being thoroughly cleaned and disinfected. Makeshift showers were set up and a portable machine brought in to fumigate our dirty old ragged clothing, while we showered a few at a time. But the most joyful and least expected news of all time was that two of the prisoners had received letters from their people in England and three other boys had received word from the British Red Cross, informing them of food and comfort packages that were being sent to them.

Although most of us were not aware of it until now, some of the prisoners had been permitted, months before when they were first captured, to fill in the answers to prepared questions printed on special POW postal cards. This could mean but one thing. The Germans had decided, after almost a year, to either make this an open registered camp, or to send us to one that was; otherwise, they never would have allowed those POW cards to leave Germany.

Only men who have lived through months of hunger, misery, torment, and fear, after being sentenced to death and then given a reprieve just minutes before the execution was to have taken place, could ever realize or fully appreciate the overwhelming sense of relief and emotion that such news could bring. When the two prisoners read aloud portions of their precious letters, I saw some of the most stout-hearted among us hurry outside to hide their tears. The knowledge that those letters were written to boys we scarcely knew and were from people we had never seen or even heard of before mattered not one iota. That was the one night in that horrible prison shack when hope and expectation became powerful enough to overcome and replace the pangs of hunger — the yearning and craving for food temporarily subsided.

A senior officer had been placed in overall command of the prison camp while I was in solitary, but the *Field Webel* was still there when I returned. Although he never spoke a word as the guard escorted me into the prison compound, I felt certain, from the intense hostile scowl on his ugly face, that he had found out about the complaint that Brown and I had made to the front-line Prussian commander during our attempted escape the month before. We later learned that this was indirectly the cause for his demotion. The day following my return to the slave camp, I was sent back to my old job, chopping down and stripping the branches from willow trees and helping to carry the heavier ones to the canal bank, from where some other prisoners placed them together with huge bundles of brushwood in the construction of the dam.

I had chopped down and trimmed the branches from a fairly large willow tree, and with the aid of two carrying cross-sticks, one underneath each end, three other prisoners and I lifted the log to take it to the canal bank. The end I was on was much too heavy for the weaker boy on the opposite end of my stick, so we set the log back on the ground in order to readjust the carrying sticks and thus distribute the weight so that the weaker prisoner would have less of the load. I was keenly aware of the *Field Webel* standing only a few yards away and watching every move we made, like a hawk. Convinced that this big, depraved brute was mentally deranged and fearing for my life, I did everything humanly possible not to displease him. We got the log up again, but it was still much too heavy for the weaker boy and he buckled under the weight. Having no other alternative, we set the log back on the ground for a second time.

This appeared to be the precise opportunity that the *Field Webel* had been waiting for. Ranting and raving like the mad man he was, he demanded to know what all the playing around was about. No one spoke. The fact was that we were all too much in fear of him to say anything. Then, as I knew he would, he asked me directly what the trouble was. I tried to tell him (what he of course already knew) that the poor lad on the other end of my stick was much too ill and weak to carry such a heavy load, but the miserable, merciless lunatic did not want the truth — he wanted only to get even with me — and him getting even, I felt sure, meant the end for me.

Shouting his wrath, he ordered us to pick the log up and take it to the canal, warning us of what would happen if we let it down again. When we placed the carrying sticks farther back, so that the two boys in the front would bear more of the load, he demanded we put them back again, compelling the weak boy to bear as much weight as before. I nudged up close to the log, trying to take over every ounce of weight I could, but it was still too heavy for the weaker boy, and after taking a few steps forward, he stumbled and fell. Although the evil, insane brute was a monster, he was nevertheless intelligent, cunning, and resourceful, knowing exactly how to go about getting the things he wanted. I was convinced that what he wanted above all other things was to get rid of me, and not just for the time being, but for all time.

Lacking any plausible excuse to attack me directly, he picked up the small limb that I had previously cut from the tree and began beating the weaker prisoner across the back because he said there was nothing wrong with the Englander swine, other than he was just too lazy and disobedient to do as he was told. Being well aware of the evil intent he had in mind, I turned my head pretending not to be at all concerned, but I was not fooling this big, crafty Prussian gorilla — not even a little bit. He knew that if he kept on beating the prisoner long enough, I would eventually work up sufficient courage or my temper would flare up and overcome my fear, compelling me to interfere by coming to the boy's rescue.

But in his eagerness for revenge, he never took the time to consider just what the other two prisoners may or may not do when they saw one of their fellow prisoners being tortured. For the rest of his life, he must have regretted his neglect, for not only did it deprive him of the sweet and pleasant revenge that he had so anxiously and passionately anticipated, it afforded me an extra sixty-five years or more to live … and hate him.

One of the two prisoners at the front end of the yellow log happened to be the Irish New Zealander — the boy responsible for the Belgian national anthem episode on the train from Dendermonde eight or more months before — and aside from having every bit as much temper as I did, he had plenty of guts to go with it. To give the devil his due, I doubt if the *Field Webel* intended to hurt the lad much, as he was not hitting him hard and there was considerable pause between blows, but the last time he swung the stick, the prisoner either ducked or stumbled, and the stick caught him directly across the mouth, causing him to cry out in pain. The New Zealander immediately leaped over the log, pushed the prisoner out of danger, and began telling the big, fat, cowardly bully what he thought of him.

The *Field Webel*, taken by complete surprise from this unexpected quarter and already overcome with hostility, went stark mad. Foaming at the mouth, he threw away the smaller stick and picked up another twice the size and began to rain blows on the New Zealander with all his might. I felt sure that in his state of mind, he would never let up until the prisoner was either dead, or like the Bantam several months before, too badly hurt to survive. I kept hoping and praying that one or more of the guards who hated this brutal Frankenstein almost as much as we did would find the moral courage to come to our aid, but none of them did. What was wrong with those German soldiers? I was certain we had the sympathy of most of them, as they had shown it many times, yet they could stand there and watch one or all of us being beaten to death by this madman, without lifting a finger to help us. In our regiment, such an officer would have been attacked before he had struck a second blow.

I realized that if I did nothing to prevent the New Zealander from a cruel beating and perhaps death and I later managed to get away from there alive, it would be like my friend Brown had remarked a month or six weeks before, when I wanted to give myself up in order to get help for him — I would never be able to live with myself after. The only alternative open to me, though [I was] shaking with fear, was to jump over the log and try to wrestle the stick from his grasp. As I did so, it brought some of his yellow-bellied guards at the double, not to help us, but to protect this crazy murdering madman from a couple of helpless and defenceless prisoners. This was not at all what he wanted and he foamed at them to stand aside.

In the meantime, he was looking around the tree stump for what I thought was another stick, but instead came up with the axe that I had previously used to chop down the tree. He made a vicious swing at me, and in trying to get away from him, I fell backwards over the log, which probably saved my life. The axe missed my head and body but cut clear through the front part of my left foot, severing one toe completely and cleaving a wide-open gash for about three inches diagonally across my foot. Thankfully, before he could swing a second time, someone had snatched the axe from his grasp.

Due to so much excitement, I had not noticed at first who was responsible for saving my life and took it for granted that one of the guards had found the courage to do so, but fortunately for me, the newly appointed commandant was on one of his routine inspection tours, arriving just in time to prevent my being hacked to pieces. The *Field Webel*, still furious and now frightened, attempted to tell his side of the story first, but he was ordered to shut up and to consider himself under arrest. The New Zealander, although badly cut about the face and bleeding quite freely, could still move about, as could the weaker prisoner, who was not seriously hurt. I never saw any of the prisoners at that slave camp again, but I did hear from the New Zealander about three or four months later, who wrote me from a POW camp in Munich.

The new commandant listened to the prisoners' version of the incident first, then checked with the guards who, now that the *Field Webel* had gone, were no longer afraid to substantiate everything the prisoners had told him. They volunteered a whole lot more on their own. The guards bandaged up my foot as best they could, constructed a makeshift lifter from some willow limbs laced with pieces of rope, and carried me to the main road, where I was loaded onto one of the trucks and driven to a hospital back at the same army base that I had left only the week before, after sweating out twenty-eight long days and nights of solitary confinement.

The doctor who operated on my foot was not unfriendly. I was given a nice clean bed [and] the same food as the sick and wounded German soldiers got, but unfortunately, I was only permitted to remain there a few days. Later in the week, I was sent to a prison camp in or near a town named Grafenwohr.[2] The accommodations there were not too bad, but the food was not better than at the slave camp, except that there was a little more of it. I was told that there had been some British prisoners there, but they had recently been transferred to other camps in Bavaria. As a result, I never heard another word of English for almost two months.

A few days after I left there, Ludendorff's storm troopers[3] broke through our supposedly impregnable defence lines, advanced a full forty miles in just one week, and captured another 125,000 British soldiers on the way, which not only refilled the Grafenwohr camp with British prisoners, but resulted in every POW camp in Germany being overcrowded for the remainder of the war.

This so-called prisoner of war hospital bore no resemblance whatever to a real hospital. It was just a long frame shack. There was no German staff, not even a doctor. Except for a wonderful little Roman Catholic sister who came in each day, the prisoners more or less took care of themselves. A civilian doctor came up from town about once in every two weeks. He glanced at a few of the worst cases occasionally, but I never saw him do anything to help them. The few prisoners that where operated on, including me, were taken to a soldier's military hospital, but the day following the operation, except in very serious cases, we were sent back to the hut.

Except for a dozen or more French prisoners who did the cooking and more or less ran the place, most of the other prisoners — particularly so the poor Russians, whose government had either forgotten all about them or no longer cared — were on the verge of starvation. Most of them had taken ill while working on German farms in and around the neighbourhood. From the little I understood, their whole ambition was to get well enough to go back to these farms again, where they had been better fed and cared for.

There were about eighty prisoners at Grafenwohr POW camp then. Half or more of them, including all the French, were receiving help from home and were in fair to good condition. The remaining half, being solely dependent on the very small, poorly prepared food allotted them by the

German government, were on the verge of starvation. But for the super-human effort of this saintly little Roman Catholic nun, all would have died there. This tiny woman, after administering to these poor miserable prisoners from eight to twelve hours each day (including Sundays), went out among the town folk at night to solicit and beg a little extra food and medicine to give them the next day.

In my eyes, never in all history has any humanitarian worked harder or given more of himself to their fellow man than did this frail-looking, petite, unassuming woman. Christ, whose teachings she so strictly adhered to, possessed no greater love or compassion. They called her a sister of mercy, but she was more than that — she was everybody's sister, mother, and friend, and I have always remembered her as a sister of pure love and devotion. If, as she so firmly believed, there is a life hereafter, this little Christ-like woman is now enjoying a deep and full divine recognition.

Nobody at this so-called prison hospital could speak a word of English. As the two or three elderly guards seldom if ever came inside the hut, the only German I ever heard was when the little sister brought me a bit of extra food. About the second or third morning after my arrival there, she came over to my bed. After looking all around to make sure that none of the guards were near the doors or windows, she produced a hard-boiled egg from a pocket somewhere inside her cape, peeling it quickly and taking every precaution to return each scrap of shell back inside her cape as though it were of great value. Then, with a coverlet held in front of her, as if about to tidy up my bed, she made me eat the egg as quickly as I could.

This same routine took place somewhere inside the hut every morning. There must have been five of us she considered to be in more weakened condition than the others, as my turn came every fifth morning. The more I thought about it, the more convinced I became that the egg smuggled to one or the other of us each morning was a sacrifice of her own breakfast. One morning, after making sure that no one could overhear and using almost as much sign language as German, I asked her if this were so. She just smiled and hastened to put me off, saying something like, "It matters not where it comes from, you just eat it and get well again," which I continued to do, but not without a twinge of conscience and a rather guilty, kind of choked-up feeling.

Two months later, when I was in a much better POW camp, I learned that the minimum penalty for giving or selling items such as cheese, sugar, or eggs to a prisoner of war was a six-month jail term. This was why the saintly little sister had taken such pains in returning all the bits of incriminating evidence back inside her cape. These six-month jail terms applied also to women and girls who become pregnant by POWs that were sent out to work on their farms. Such warnings or threats had little or no effect, and I doubt if they were meant to be taken too seriously — at least not in that part of Germany, because there were hundreds, perhaps thousands, of such cases.

———

After making a partial recovery from foot surgery, Manuel is transferred to the larger Ingolstadt POW camp for the war's duration.[4] This camp had better food and accommodations. Most of its POWs were British Empire prisoners. As a registered POW, Manuel now receives Red Cross care packages. Manuel is so weak when he arrives that doctors warn him eating too much food could easily kill him.

———

About two months after being admitted to the Grafenwohr prison camp on a day in late spring, the little sister came in, and when she had washed my face, straightened my bed up a bit, and given me the last precious egg that I would ever receive from her, she informed me that later in the morning, an English-speaking doctor would be coming to see me. I could sense by the look on his face when he saw me that he was very much surprised to see something still alive that looked so awful dead. After a most thorough check, he smiled and said, "When I was a medical student in Heidelberg, we had someone there who looked a lot like you." I replied, "Yes, I know — a skeleton."

If he resented my taking the punch from his joke, he showed no sign of it and laughed long and loud. He held the rank of major or the German equivalent. I saw him quite often during the months that followed and got to like him very much and so did all of the other prisoners. He would be classed as a real gentleman in any civilized country — the kind of man the boys back in the regiment would refer to as a "good Joe." He never talked down to the prisoners, nor demanded that they snap to attention and salute every time he passed by, which accounted for his being shown as much friendly respect by both the prisoners and his own men as any officer I ever knew — either inside Germany or out.

Before leaving to examine some other prisoners, he asked if I thought I could stand a three- or four-hour car ride. I assured him I could if someone would carry me to the car. During the past two weeks, my foot had swollen to almost twice its normal size, and because it felt so very painful, I was afraid it had become blood poisoned and so did the little sister, which was no doubt the reason for persuading the Ingolstadt commandant to send a doctor in the first place. How she ever managed to do so, I don't know, but if miracles are wrought by faith, then that saintly little woman possessed all the necessary qualifications.

The major said he was taking me to Ingolstadt, where I would meet and be with other British Empire prisoners. The little sister helped me on with my old tattered uniform, wrapped a blanket around my shoulders, and asked one of the guards to carry me to the car. This he willingly did, as soon as I had thanked and said goodbye to one of the most humane, unselfish, self-sacrificing women in all time, and if that beautiful song about "wanting to be in that number when the saints go marching in" has substance, she won't be just one of their numbers when they march in, she will be leading them.

It was a most beautiful spring day, with all the shrubs and flowers in full bloom. The major drove the car himself and kept up a friendly conversation all the way. For me, it was a most pleasant journey, and despite the pain in my injured foot, I enjoyed every moment of it. We arrived at the camp in the late afternoon, stopping at what appeared to be the staff office. The major spoke with the corporal of the guard for a moment or two, then, as though talking to an honoured guest rather than a despised prisoner of war, he asked me to wait in the car for a few more minutes while he went inside to make some inquiries.

About ten minutes later, a couple of German soldiers came out and took a look at me inside the car. One of them turned to his comrade and commented, "God in Himmel, Hans! This Englander is just a heap of bones and weighs less than a baby!" and so saying, he reached in and picked me up as though I was just that — a baby. And while Hans (as he called him) followed along behind, he carried me down through a long, narrow corridor and into a very small but clean, bright, and sunny room at the far end of the building. The bunk bed had an old-fashioned feather mattress, the first I had seen since leaving home almost four years before. Although such beds are considered by some of the medical experts to be unhealthy and bad for the posture, I could remember people who had slept on them every night for as long as ninety years, or longer, having kept themselves strong, healthy, and contented throughout a long life of toil and hardship. Healthy or not, this one sure looked good to me after the bulky lump of straw I had just left and the many worse ones (or none at all) before that.

Hans helped his friend in removing my old tunic and trousers, and as I was still wearing the second-hand suit of charity pyjamas that the little sister had begged for from someone downtown, I was ready for bed in record time. I no longer possessed any shoes, and if I did, I could have worn only one. There was one consolation in owning so little — one was always free from the fear of being robbed. It would be both illegal and immoral to be seen in public with as little to cover one's nakedness as I possessed at this time. One of the soldiers fetched me a pitcher of nice cold water, and after saying something about the doctor coming soon, they both returned to their regular routine.

The major came in an hour or so later and took another look at my foot. Despite his assurance that everything would turn out all right and the professional, noncommittal expression on his face, I sensed that he had his doubts as to whether my foot could be saved or not. This doubt, which he admitted to a month or so later, had kept me awake all night. I was taken to the people's hospital downtown early next morning. I saw the major there, but a civilian doctor performed the operation. He was a very unpleasant man, or, at least, he was unpleasant with me. He did not condescend to speak, but he gave me a look of scornful contempt as though I was just another kind of slimy slug that had crawled out from beneath a rock in his garden. I soon realized that he was just another of those English-hating Prussians who would have been delighted to see all of them looking as I did. He did not permit his hostility to prevent him from doing an excellent job on my foot, however. For that, I was very, very grateful, although he never gave me a chance to tell him so.

I was back in my little room again before the effects of the anesthetic wore off. I had no idea how long I had been back or how I got there, but when I turned back the blanket and saw that my foot was still attached to my leg, I could have actually gone back and bear-hugged that English-hating surgeon, had it been possible. The major came to see me again before leaving for Bayreuth next day. He was pleased about the operation and told me how lucky I was to have one of the best surgeons in Germany to perform the procedure. "Your greatest danger now," he said, "is not your foot, but the generosity of your British comrades." He told me that seven or eight weeks before, a dozen prisoners from the very camp where I had worked behind the line were transferred to a POW camp near Munich. "They were just skeletons like yourself," [he said], but because their friends, who received many good items from the British Red Cross, had fed them too much of the rich food too soon, four of them had died and two others were dangerously ill.[5]

Shortly after the major left, two English prisoners came in, and, except for the fact that a stripe of brownish material extended down the outside of the trouser legs and another around one sleeve of the coat of their well-tailored blue serge suits, they could easily have been mistaken for a couple of well-dressed businessmen. I was amazed; never had I expected to see anything like this inside Germany. They were both in the very pink of condition, with full faces and rosy cheeks, wearing nice blue bonnets and newly shined shoes. They appeared to me at the time as though they might have been chosen by one of London's finest clothing establishments to model the style of suit the well-dressed young men would be wearing that season.

I was so surprised at what I was seeing that I actually forgot to greet them as soon or as courteously as I would otherwise have done, for which I later apologized. One was the RAMC[6] sergeant that the major had consulted about taking care of me. The other lad (I think his name was Sloan) was from Yorkshire. They were both very good-looking young men. I kept staring at them because what I saw was so pleasing to the eye, while they, in turn (as they both admitted to me some weeks later), were so nauseated by my ugly spook-like appearance that neither had enjoyed his dinner that evening. They had both been prisoners much longer than I had, but like the vast majority of British POW camps where Red Cross assistance was already available, they had never seen a prisoner from one of those behind-the-lines slave labour camps before, only having heard rumours of such places.

Although it took just about every ounce of willpower I possessed, I did manage to wait until the two prisoners had left for their own quarters before eating anything from the little box of mouth-watering food they had brought me. The box contained a cup of beef broth, three soda biscuits, two very thin slices of white Swiss bread with just a token of butter spread, and a California orange. Except for the few hard-boiled eggs smuggled to me by the saintly Roman Catholic sister at the Grafenwohr hospital and the tin of blood sausage that Brown and I stole from the deserted farmhouse on our three-day journey to the German front line during our attempted escape from the slave labour camp several months before, this comprised just about all of the real nourishing food that I had eaten in over nine months.

Although more than sixty years have come and gone since I consumed that small portion of delicious food and the many others that followed during my seven weeks of isolation in that tiny room, never before nor since (and I have dined in some of the best restaurants, occasionally, both here in Ontario and across the river in the U.S.A.?) have I eaten anything that tasted quite as good or gave so much pleasure and enjoyment in the eating.

My little room was located at the far end of a long, narrow, enclosed corridor, with perhaps a half dozen or more doors leading into other rooms, including the guards' quarters. Early in the afternoon of my second day there, I was awakened by a kind of scraping noise, as if a heavily loaded wheelbarrow was being pushed down the corridor just outside my room with its sides rubbing against both walls, followed by running footsteps together with very high-pitched voices shouting in German, "Nein, nein, nix, nix, Englander, you cannot go in there, it is forbidden, you must have a pass, you will be put in the guardhouse!" etc.

Then, in a loud, clear voice that was undoubtedly North American, "You damn fool German krauts! What in hell makes you so stupid? How bloody often have I told you that I am not an Englander, I am a Canadian! If

I was an Englander, chances are I could be some kin to you crazy mixed-up Germans, and if I thought for one minute that I was related to any of your square-headed Deutschlanders, I would grab one of those antique blowguns you have there but don't know how to shoot with, and I would immediately blow my brains out right here and now in this damn crazy dungeon tunnel, which is too bloody narrow to get my wheelchair through!"

The voice continued with vim and vigour. How much, if any, the poor guards understood of so much dialogue, I have no idea, but he sure managed to bring them around to his way of thinking. Never before had I seen or heard of anything to compare to what I witnessed that afternoon; instead of taking orders from his captors, he was giving them, and the most surprising part of all, they apparently enjoyed doing exactly as he ordered because when he called for one of them to come and take him out about two hours later, all three of them came rushing in, vying with each other for the privilege of carrying him out to his wheelchair.

I met and got to know two prisoners in Germany who apparently could get away with just about anything short of murder. One was an Irishman from Dublin or somewhere near there and the other was this big good-looking Canadian, or rather, he had been big before he lost his legs. His name was Jack Crowe and he was from Owen Sound, Ontario.[8] When the Germans found him out in no man's land, where he had lain for a couple of days and nights, his one leg was off and the other so badly shattered that it had to be immediately amputated. To have survived out there for so long in such a terrible condition must have called for super-human strength and endurance. This, of course, accounts for the fact that he could do or say just about as he pleased.

Most Germans, being courageous and enduring themselves (and I take issue with anyone who says otherwise), admire the same trait in others. They may dislike or even hate the British during wartime because the Germans never seem to have any luck in winning that last and final battle; nevertheless, deep within (and begrudgingly, maybe), there is considerable admiration and respect for the stamina and fortitude of the Anglo-Saxon people.

Like me, Jack loved the water — particularly so the Great Lakes. He never grew tired of expounding the magnificent scenery in and around the Bruce Peninsula and Georgian Bay where he had lived, fished, and hunted. Since then, I have made many trips up there during the summer months and found it to be every bit as beautiful as he claimed it was. The scenery in and around those Thirty Thousand Islands[9] being so pictur-esque and breathtaking as to be almost unbelievable, one unsurpassed anywhere else in North America.

About eight weeks later, when they permitted me to join the other prisoners over in the British compound, I got my first look at Jack's wheel-chair and could readily see why it had given him so much trouble in the narrow corridor. The wheels were at least eight inches farther apart than they should have been. His friends had put it together with just sufficient clearance to pass through the door opening of the hut where Jack lived, which happened to be one of the widest in the whole compound. It was rather a crude-looking outfit; nevertheless, it served its purpose. Some of the guards had donated the parts and supplied the tools to put it together.

One afternoon, when Jack took off to visit some bedridden prisoners whose hut was several hundred feet away with rather a steep downgrade at the far end, some German men and women working on the land outside the compound waved their hands in greeting as they usually did when he passed by. Unfortunately, while Jack was returning the compliment by waving back at them, his chair had approached the downgrade, and before he could get his hands back on the wheels in order to check its momentum, it had gained so much extra speed as to be completely out of control and heading straight for the barbed wire enclosure.

Had he clashed with it, it would almost certainly have cut him up badly. The guards and everyone else who saw it were much concerned for his safety, but while Jack had lost control of his wheelchair, he was still in full control of his wits, and now being well aware of the inevitable, he pushed himself out over the side of the chair and began rolling along behind it like a big rubber ball, coming to a complete stop within about ten feet of the ugly and dangerous barbed wire....

Unfortunately, not yet being able to make it outside on my injured foot, I missed the excitement, but heard all about it from one of the prisoners — an eyewitness who told me that although some of the British prisoners were as close to Jack when the accident occurred as the Germans were and ran as fast as they could to his rescue, the guards reached him first, carried him over to their own quarters, and fed him all the schnapps he could drink until a doctor from downtown came to look him over. Although he suffered no serious injury, he was ordered to rest up in bed for at least a week. I think the doctor was more concerned about the stub of his left leg, which had become ulcerated several times since the amputation.

Because of his love for the outdoors, it was nigh to impossible to keep him in bed long enough for his stubs to heal. The English RAMC sergeant, who knew much about such things, was constantly pleading with him to slow down and take it easy and often warned him of serious complications ahead unless he took better care of himself. It was the same after he came home to Canada. I remember back in the twenties, when we were both patients at Christie Street Hospital in Toronto,[10] often against the advice of his doctors, he would strap on his two artificial legs and take off downtown. The constant friction and irritation of those artificial legs coming into contact with his very sore and tender stubs must have inflicted intense pain with every step he took, but apparently, he would rather suffer the pain than spend all of his days cooped up inside. He was always on the go at the prison camp, visiting the sick and wounded, and particularly so those who had become depressed or demoralized.

Jack, like me, had very little schooling. He would much rather go fishing than go to school. That was too bad because, with a good education, he could have been anything he desired to be. Even without it, he did as well or perhaps better than many professional psychologists could have done under similar conditions. One of the methods he used to boost the morale and restore self-confidence to some of the poor boys who were already demoralized was to start a debate or an argument or have someone else start it for him and then take the opposite position to that of the boy he was trying to help. He would do anything to get the man in question out of his shell and interested enough to take part in the discussion.

Many of the prisoners on the verge of a nervous breakdown, if not completely cured, were at least helped in this way. This seemed especially so for the countless teenagers of which, during the last two years of the slaughter, there were great numbers from both sides — boys who should have been back home attending school instead of being compelled by the greedy empire expansionists to kill each other.

I recall that about six weeks before the war ended, Jack went to plead with the camp commandant not to send the two seventeen-year-old youths (who had suddenly become unmanageable) to the dreaded mental POW prison that we had heard so many bad things about.[11] The commandant was one of the most humane and sympathetic officers on either side of the line and a real gentleman in every sense of the word. He never sent any of the deranged prisoners to the cruel insane asylum, unless to protect the other prisoners and his men and left with no other alternative. He agreed to postpone sending the two deranged boys away, providing Jack could guarantee that a sufficient number of able-bodied prisoners would always be close by and on call to restrain and take care of the two unfortunate youths, should the need arise — a guarantee Jack found quite easy to give, as there were enough volunteers within ten minutes of his asking to take care of the two insane lads for several years.

Whether or not the two poor boys ever recovered after making it back home to England I have no idea, but their people would have Jack to thank for keeping them out of that horrible lunatic prison that we had heard so many terrifying stories about (although I have no direct personal experience of such a place, nor did I ever talk with anyone who had actually been there).

During the week that Jack was confined to his bed, the guards, with the consent and goodwill of the commandant no doubt, had taken his wheelchair to a machine shop downtown. When he got it back a couple of weeks later, it looked like a brand-new model. They had taken about six inches from the width, installed handbrakes, and added a padded seat and fresh coat of a pretty beige shade paint.

I never saw a man — not even one in possession of all of his limbs — who was more active, vigorous, and full of life than Jack was. Despite all of his hardships and suffering, I never once saw him discouraged or feeling sorry for himself, nor did he ever complain of his terrible handicap. He lived through and beyond middle age, which surprised most of his friends — particularly so his doctors who were constantly warning him that unless he slowed down and took better care of himself, he would likely be found dead in the street one day. Although he never got to hunt much again, his Owen Sound friends made sure he went on as many fishing trips as he cared to. Jack was the only POW I ever saw after leaving Germany. We met again in the middle twenties at the old Christie Street Hospital in Toronto where we were both patients for almost a year.

The officer in charge of the mail and censorship department at this huge prison camp was a captain who had lost an arm at the front. He had no direct contact with the prisoners unless one of us was called to explain a sentence or paragraph in a letter we had written to our people or friends back home. His staff took care of all of our letters and Red Cross packages; however, he must have seen (or one of his staff must have told him) that all of the food parcels addressed to me were being sent by the Canadian Red Cross society.

One morning, about two or three months before the war ended and about a week or two after my foot had healed enough to bear some weight, another prisoner and I walked over to the postal depot to ask if any mail had come for either of us or for another prisoner who was still confined to his bunk, suffering from influenza (which was just beginning to spread all through the camp). I was told by the man at the desk to wait awhile. A minute or two later, a captain came out from his office carrying my Red Cross package over one arm and holding it steady with the stub of the other. "So you are Canadian," he greeted me in flawless English, and for the reason already mentioned, I said yes. He asked me, "Did you by any chance take part in the Battle of Courcelette in September 1916?" To that, of course, I had to say no.[12]

"Well," he said, pointing to his empty sleeve, "one of your boys gave me this and they damn near wiped out my whole battalion. It was our first tangle with the Canadians. We had known for some time that they were preparing to attack us, but our commanding officer assured us that, as they were just a mixture of untrained, undisciplined woodsmen and farmers, we had nothing whatever to worry about. From what he had heard, he was certain that, as soon as we had repulsed the first line or wave, all the others would turn tail, take flight, and run like the same number of scared rabbits. The CO was quite right about the Canadians running like rabbits, but unfortunately for our regiment, they ran in the wrong direction, and when we were forced to run, they insisted on running after us ...

"Three times that day, we felt sure we had them stopped, but each time, they rallied. Those Canadian boys were out to win that day and win they did. Nothing short of sufficient men and guns to drop each and every man before he reached our front trench could have prevented them from doing so. They may have been amateurs, but no professionals ever fought better. Our colonel was in much better spirits when about a month or so later, he was granted leave to visit his wife and family and took time out to come and see me at the hospital. Instead of being reprimanded (as, for some unknown reason, I felt sure he thought he would be), he was highly commended for his very efficient leadership in taking personal charge of his officers and men and in regrouping a second time at the support trench, thus gaining enough extra time for sufficient reinforcements to reach and secure the third trench against a most determined and worthy foe...."

All through the captain's story, I felt rather guilty and embarrassed, as though I was actually stealing something sacred from the many courageous young men he was praising so highly. He readily understood, however, when I explained why I was passing as a Canadian. Yes, he knew well enough where Newfoundland was located, but he always thought that everything north of the United States was part of Canada, all of which was owned and governed by England's king and parliament, and at that time, well over 99 percent of all Europeans thought as he did — and for that matter, the majority of them still do. How could they think otherwise when for over a hundred years after Confederation, Canadian ships were still sailing in and out of every known port on the globe flying another people's flag, and they would be doing so yet, but for the perseverance and determination of Lester (Mike) Pearson, who, despite the long and bitter opposition from so many Ottawa politicians, did finally succeed in giving us a flag of our own.[13] Some of the smart boys made jokes about it and dubbed it the distress signal — the half-mast flag — Pearson's pennant, etc., but most people I know think it is a beautiful flag and so do I.

The one-armed captain was not boasting when he said his men had put up a good fight, and the Canadian boys who fought them would be among the first to agree. A German soldier always fought well, not because he possessed any more courage than a British soldier, but because he was better trained, better led, and had far more confidence in the men who planned and directed his battles. The fact that they lost the war had nothing whatever to do with it. We would have lost it long before they did if we had been compelled to fight on as many fronts with so few men as they had. All of those ridiculous, fictitious press reports during the first year or two of the war about the German soldier fighting well only when he was surrounded by his friends or driven by his officers was just so much bunk, written by a bunch of irresponsible, base-located reporters, none of whom had ever been within twenty miles of the fighting front.

If the German soldier lacked courage, why did it take us so long to win the war and why, for every 100 German soldiers killed on the British sector of the Western Front, did we lose 250? — a ratio of two and one-half to one. That is the official figure, but my guess would be closer to twice that number. When Germany first asked for an armistice in 1918, after defeating the great Russian Empire and a couple of smaller nations, she held more conquered territory than at any time during the war, and her enemies were farther from her borders than ever before. Germany lost the war because, owing to the 100 percent stranglehold by the British, French, and finally American navies, she no longer possessed the means to continue fighting.

Some of her people (particularly so the working-class German people) were already on a slow starvation diet, existing on less than half of the number of calories required for an adult person. If they weren't such a tough, enduring people, their government would have been compelled to sue for peace at least a year before they did. Most of the civilian population were living on nothing more than sauerkraut, turnip, and potatoes (which they were forbidden to peel before cooking), plus a fair-sized mouthful of pork once each week.

There had already been one serious crop failure during the war years; a second would have spelled total disaster for the common people. Like thousands of poor, wretched, miserable Russians over in the adjoining prison compounds, they too would have died of starvation. During the last two years of the war, everything in the line of food had been reduced to a mere pittance until coffee, sugar, butter, and meat (except the three-inch square of pork each week) were only luxuries of the past. I often wondered if our own people would have stood for such strict regimentation and hardships without kicking over the traces.

While I had never been inside a German home or worked on any of their farms, I talked with a number of prisoners who had. The stories they told me regarding the people's food rations (except in a few isolated cases where the farmer had defied the authorities in converting a pig or a few chicken to his own use) were exactly the same in every detail, as if told over and over again by the very same person. The German family menu never changed from one day to the next, except on Thursdays when their small weekly allowance of pork was added to the cabbage or sauerkraut and cooked much longer than in pre-war days, in order to give the meal a more meaty or greasy flavour.

For breakfast, they ate a thick sticky porridge — in most cases without milk or sweetening of any kind. It consisted mainly of coarsely ground grain — the kind generally used to feed cattle — but containing a special ingredient the prisoners contended was a certain kind of wood sawdust imported from Turkey and supposedly full of nutrition and vitamins. It was also used to fortify the stone-heavy, black war bread, and it never lost its drab grey colour in the mixing and baking. That was exactly what it looked like — a sprinkling of greyish-white sawdust all through the loaves of black breads.

With the very unappetizing porridge, they ate some dry black war bread, washing it down with a substitute coffee made from burnt, diced *mangelwurzel,* a kind of beetroot. For the noonday meal, there was a thick potato soup, boiled unskinned potatoes, sauerkraut or cabbage, more black bread, and frequently a pickled herring. For dessert, there was usually raw fruit such as an apple, plum, or pear, depending on what was in season. Owing to the shortage of sweetening, there was seldom if ever any kind of jams, jellies, or prepared fruits. There is no need for my listing or itemizing the evening meal because it was identical with the one at noon, with just one exception — it was minus the pickled herring.

When I had been in that little room for about a week, the oldest soldier I ever saw came to see me. He brought me one of Charles Dickens's novels, which I had read years before, but I was delighted to read it again. He told me his name was McNeil from Glasgow, Scotland, and he was sixty-one years old. He had, of course, like thousands of others either too young or too old for military service when war broke out, lied about his age, but this old chap must have been the most convincing liar in all time if he had satisfied the doctors at the recruiting centre of not being many years over the age limit. Here he was, having been wounded and captured on the Passchendaele front two years before and less than a thousand yards from where I was captured a full sixteen months later. This should serve to give the reader some idea of the very small progress made in two full years of wholesale slaughter in the blood-soaked Passchendaele mud.

There were other blessings to be thankful for now. It was along about this time that I received my first letter from home in reply to a form card that I had been permitted to send from the Grafenwohr camp three or more months before. This was the first my people knew of me being a prisoner — the only news they had received previously being one of those chilly precise telegrams from the establishment: "We regret to inform you that your son has been reported missing and believed killed in action."

A few days later came a twelve-pound package of delicious canned foods from the Canadian Red Cross people, followed by one containing a POW uniform, undergarments, a pair of shoes, toothbrush and paste, a cake of soap (which was worth its weight in gold in parts of Germany at that time), plus several other personal items, all of which I was in dire need of. From then until war's end, I received a food parcel at regular intervals from the Canadian Red Cross people to which I have always been deeply indebted and forever grateful. Although I never lost hope of getting out of Germany alive, it is questionable as to whether I could have survived the last six months of the war without their help, and the same could be said for a half million or more other British Empire prisoners as well. A considerable number of extra packages addressed to prisoners who had died of their wounds or from other causes since coming to the camp were opened up and the contents divided equally among the Italians and other Allied prisoners, with some being held in reserve to take care of newly captured Empire prisoners.

The Americans had been fighting on the Western Front for some time when I came to this camp.[14] Shortly after some of them had been captured and assigned to our section of the camp (and in order to take care of them until such time as their own government or Red Cross could make contact, which usually took about two to three months), a prisoner from Britain and one from each of the dominions were selected to supervise the sharing of our food parcels with them and they were given the same amount of the same items as we kept for ourselves.

I shall never forget, within about ten or twelve weeks later, some of them received their very first packages from the American Red Cross

— huge boxes filled with such luxuries as canned lobster, bacon and eggs, shrimp, jams, real butter, cigarettes, giant-sized chocolate bars, and more. Well, these American boys were so excited and so filled with gratitude for the way the British prisoners had (in some cases) gone short themselves in order to give them an equal share that if we had let them, they would have given every precious thing away, and despite all the opposition, they insisted on sharing their most prized items — the chocolate bars and cigarettes. When they had given each prisoner in our section of the compound one cigarette and one-third of a chocolate bar, they had exactly nine cigarettes and three chocolate bars left to divide up amongst the seventeen of them.

Instead of feeling sorry, I felt proud for them because I knew that this was precisely the way they wanted it to be. Having something to give rather than being obliged to take all the time had given them a mighty lift and boosted their morale sky-high. Persuading others to take the very sweet meats and delicacies that one's own body is craving for means something far different than just giving something that one can quite easily do without, and by doing so, those boys had made a real sacrifice, which accounted for the glow in their cheeks and that unmistakable look of self-respect and well-being.

Well over 90 percent of British Empire prisoners at this camp were from the British Isles, about two hundred or more were from Australia, and perhaps half that number were from New Zealand. Three of the older men, one Irish and two English, were the only professional peacetime soldiers at the camp. They had been captured way back in 1914, during the retreat from Mons, four years less three months before, and because of the kaiser's scornful remark referring to them as that contemptible little army, all of its members have been known ever since as the "Old Contemptibles."[15] Although, I have read several times since that the kaiser never said any such thing — that the English said it for him — which is very likely, as the English were tops at that kind of propaganda (although they, too, goofed occasionally).

Somewhere around the latter part of August or early September 1918, the major who had been so kind to me informed me of plans that were being negotiated in Switzerland for an exchange of a hundred or more disabled British and German prisoners. I was to be one of the seven to go from our camp. Although he possessed no definite knowledge of just when the exchange was to take place, he had been advised by his superiors to select thirty of his worst cases and send their names (and particulars of each prisoner) to them at headquarters immediately. Only those considered no longer fit for any kind of war work could be chosen. The tremendous effect of such wonderful, unexpected news was so overwhelming as to keep me awake during the whole of that night.

Another very pleasing surprise was that my friend McNeil had been chosen as one of the lucky seven, but why or how this could be when he appeared to be in such perfect health was difficult to understand. Most of us concluded that it must be because of his age. Not until a couple of months later did we learn how grievously wrong we had been. The only one of the chosen seven to show little or no enthusiasm was the legless Jack Crowe. It was not, of course, that he did not want to go home every bit as much as the rest of us, it was that he just hated to leave his friends behind — especially so, the younger homesick boys with the low morale, the boys, he had been trying so hard to help. I never saw so many sad faces at any one time before — not even at a funeral. One poor boy broke down and sobbed, and I sensed that there were other boys, including Jack himself, who came rather close to joining him.

It was all so pitiful and, as it turned out, needless. Although we kept most of our few belongings packed, as the major had advised, in case we were obliged to leave in a hurry, we were still waiting for the order to come through on the day that the Armistice was signed, about three months later. While there were all kinds of pro and con rumours as to why they kept postponing our departure from week to week, no one at our camp seemed to know — not even the camp commandant, although he tried several times to find out. So did the major. We heard later that the sick and wounded German prisoners from Britain had been waiting in Switzerland for almost two months, but, because the British had refused to send certain prisoners that the Germans had asked for, they refused to take part in any further negotiations. Of course, that was a rumour that was likely untrue.

———

Manuel's eye for detail and his Newfoundland wit are captured in this account of the POWs' assault on the prison camp schnapps distillery.

———

One of the larger buildings on the immense prison camp farm was a distillery used for the making of schnapps, which some of the prisoners later discovered (much to their grief) was a very potent alcoholic beverage distilled from potatoes — including those unfit for any other purpose. The distillery was more or less automatic. A large chute extended through the wall to the outside. The potatoes were either dumped or shovelled from the wagons into the chute. Here, the automatic equipment took care of the actual distilling of the schnapps. When all the tanks or vats were filled with the crushed potatoes, the machinery would automatically cease operating (or, at least that was the way I visualized it from what the prisoners who had seen it told the rest of us at the camp). There may have been more to it than that.

Later, when the alcohol had matured to a certain degree, government men would come out from the city to bottle and label it. On one such trip, they were short of sufficient help to complete the work on schedule, so twelve British prisoners were sent from our camp to help them. Three of those irresponsible prisoners managed to get themselves (as well as the other nine) in a peck of trouble and came very close to having the entire British compound lose all of its hard-won privileges. Apparently, the sight of so much alcohol was too much of a temptation to resist, so they concocted a scheme to smuggle some of it back to camp. They were not satisfied with stealing just one or two bottles, so by quitting time that evening, they had somehow managed to sneak out a full twenty-four bottles of the stuff, which they hid in some rose bushes beside one of the nearby sheds. Arrangements were made with the same number of prisoners gathering the potatoes to take one bottle each with them on their way from work.

They experienced no difficulty in getting all twenty-four bottles back to camp, and if they had used some common sense in handling and drinking the stuff after they got it there, they could very well have gotten away with it. Unfortunately, they were senseless enough to open all of the two dozen bottles at once and let everyone who cared to help themselves. In less than two hours, many prisoners in the compound were cockeyed drunk. I doubt if some of the younger boys had ever drunk hard liquor before, but certainly nothing as strong and potent as that new raw, immature alcohol. Just one or two drinks and some of them were knocked out cold, leaving them unconscious and quiet until morning, but others went crazy. They sang, prayed, made speeches, and some of them had crying jags that kept the rest of us awake all night.

One young lad, who must have gone temporarily insane, ran outside and attempted to drown himself by diving headfirst into one of the huge rain barrels that had been placed at one corner of the hut to catch the water from the roof. But for that particular incident, the theft of the schnapps might never have been discovered. Fortunately for the prisoner, he was seen diving into the rain barrel by one of the guards on duty outside the prison barbed wire. Otherwise, he would have surely drowned. Even the very short time taken for the guard to open the gate, hurry inside, and pull him out came close to being too late, as he appeared quite lifeless when rescued and it took a considerable amount of resuscitation to get him breathing again.

Next morning was really the morning after. Guards with fixed bayonets were swarming all over the place. Nobody was permitted to move from beside their bunks until our entire section of the compound had been searched by both officers and guards. All twenty-four empty bottles were found and taken over to the guardhouse to be used as evidence if needed. Every prisoner in our section of the compound who was well enough to leave his bunk was escorted by armed guards over to the main building and lined up in front of the commandant's office. Over sixty years later, I cannot recall every word, but what follows is the gist of a remarkable speech.

He did not keep us waiting in suspense too long, nor did he lose his temper and rave and rant as so many of his peers were in the habit of doing even when they had less cause, or maybe no cause at all. In fact, his reprimand was surprisingly mild. He appeared to be more hurt or disappointed than angry — disappointed because he had trusted us and we had let him down. Although I was completely innocent (as were well over 98 percent of all the other prisoners in that lineup), it was the first and only time as a prisoner of war in Germany that I had felt a sense of shame, and I think most of the other prisoners who had refrained from taking any part in that disgraceful drunken orgy felt much the same way.

The commandant began by saying that, although we were British and Britain had chosen to declare war against his country, he had never personally held any ill will against prisoners of war — after all, we had only followed orders in fighting for our country the same as he and his men were doing for theirs. As to who, or which side, was right or wrong, was not the responsibility of the soldier, and to him, a prisoner captured in battle through no fault of his own was still a soldier and he respected him as such, but only as long as he behaved himself and acted as a responsible soldier should. "If German soldiers were convicted of a crime as serious as the one some of you men committed yesterday," he said, "they would be severely dealt with. In the two years that I have been in charge of this camp, I have never had cause to write or complain to my superiors of a serious charge against a British prisoner of war, but unless those of you who are actually responsible for the theft of the alcohol admit your guilt and accept the consequences, I will be obliged to do so now, in which case, all of you will suffer for the stupidity of a few.

The commandant continued in the same quiet but determined fashion. He told us that "… if I write my superiors — and I must if you give me no alternative — you will be deprived of most and perhaps all of your privileges and the whole British section of the camp will likely be placed under severe restrictions. I am not interested in knowing who drank the alcohol, perhaps some of those who did have been punished enough. In the meantime, the twelve of you who helped out in the distillery will be placed under arrest. No doubt, some of you are innocent, and if so, it's up to the guilty ones to speak up and admit it. I am not asking any of you to snitch on your friends — if they really were your friends, there would be no need or reason for you doing so…."

It continued in this line for several minutes. He said, "I have heard a great deal about British fair play and sportsmanship. You now have an excellent opportunity to show me some of it. You have until noon tomorrow, when I write my report. After that, it will in all probability be out of my hands, but I can assure you now that unless those of you who are actually responsible for stealing the schnapps report to me before then, harsh restrictions on the whole British section of the camp are bound to follow. The guards will be given orders to escort any of you to my office, anytime you decide to come and see me. In the meantime, you will all be confined to your quarters to think it over, and I hope for your own sake and for the sake of all your friends and comrades, you make the right decision, because I have been told by my superiors during and since their last two visits that half or more of you appear to them to be healthy and strong enough to perform outside manual labour. They think I am far too soft and lenient in keeping so many of you here at the camp instead of sending you out to work on the farms and in the salt mines."

Just as we were about to be dismissed, three of the prisoners stepped smartly out in front of the commandant — one of them, a real Irish wit, clicked his heels together in salute and said: "Sir, we are the three crooks who stole the hooch, but I am the one solely to blame. Those two Limeys here beside me were very much opposed to the idea and wanted no part of it, but I needed help, so I talked them into it. You know how it is with some of those weak-willed Englanders, sir," he said. "They are easily influenced and just can't say no." There were two prisoners at this camp who could get away with just about anything short of murder. The legless Jack Crowe from Owen Sound was one of them, and this ever-smiling Irishman from somewhere near Dublin was the other. True, he did not quite manage to talk himself out of this one, but he made out a great deal better than he deserved.

In addition to possessing all the so-called "luck of the Irish," he was a wit and a charmer. During his plea on behalf of his two English friends and conspirators, we all noticed the commandant turn quickly around and face his officer. Everyone was sure he did so solely to hide a smile or to keep from laughing out loud. Even the guards who understood little or no English sensed the humour of what was taking place. When he turned back and faced us, he tried hard to appear more stern and harsh. Frowning at the Irishman, he ordered him to quit talking, but before the guards took them away, he thanked all three prisoners for having the courage to admit their guilt. All the rest of us, including the other nine who helped to bottle the schnapps, were dismissed and permitted to return to our quarters without escort. We were told that, for the time being, no further restrictions would be placed on our compound and we were free to carry on as before.

Despite the fact that the majority of us took no part in the booze party and were all very angry at those who did, we could not help but feel a sense of warmth for the three prisoners who were game enough to take the much harsher punishment than any of us would have suffered by further restrictions on our compound. I am inclined to think that the commandant felt that way too, although, of course, he dared not say so. Some of us got together that afternoon and collected enough German marks to cover the cost of the schnapps, plus a slight damage to some of the bunks. Then we persuaded my friend McNeil to take it over to the commandant and express our regrets for what had happened and assure him that we would do our very best to prevent any further disturbance or rowdiness in the future.

We concluded (and rightly so, as it turned) that if everything was back to normal and operating smoothly before the three prisoners came up for sentencing on the following Thursday, the commandant might be much more inclined toward leniency. Most everyone at the camp, both friend and foe, knew and respected McNeil. He was much older than any of the other prisoners at the camp. He was also much wiser than most of us (or at least more knowledgeable). We were confident that if there was one among us capable of softening up the commandant without making it appear too obvious, McNeil was the man. The commandant talked with him for half an hour or more and requested that he thank us all for our apologies and concern. He refused to take the money we sent over, however. He stated that he did not have the authority to do so. The guards over at the jail, however, held no such qualms when we bribed them with the money, in return for their promise to help the three prisoners as much as possible during their term of solitary confinement.

The influenza epidemic struck our prison camp along about this time in 1918[16] and the prisoners began dropping and dying like many sprayed flies — particularly so, the poor starving Russians, most of whom were just fleshless skeletons of skin and bones. According to one of their guards, those in the compound at the far end of the camp died at the rate of between seven hundred and a thousand each week.

Busloads of young medical students came up from one of the universities every day to dissect the bodies and learn how to become good doctors and surgeons, for which Germany has always been famous. Most of the British prisoners were sick with it as well, but less than 2 percent of them died. One of those who did occupied a bunk next to mine, which had me scared stiff all over again and for a much longer period. No one seemed to know what it was, or from whence it came at that time, but according to the *Encyclopedia Britannica*, it's been around for thousands of years. Some of the old biblical characters are supposed to have suffered and died from its effects. My wife's sister and most of her family died of it. It killed over three million Americans and about the same number of Canadians proportionately. It wiped out whole towns and villages in parts of Eastern Europe and India.

After the doctors and students had finished dissecting and experimenting on the bodies of the Russian prisoners who had died (perhaps as much or more from hunger and starvation as from influenza), other Russian prisoners would enclose the various dissected parts into some kind of gunny sacks or burlap bags and then place the bags in the bottom of a very long, deep trench that had previously been dug and prepared for that purpose. After the bags had been placed, a few inches of earth would be thrown over them. Next day, more bodies and parts of bodies would be added and the process continued until the trench was filled. Then a new one would be dug....

# CHAPTER NINE

## ARMISTICE, NOVEMBER 1918

Manuel does not specifically recall the November 11, 1918, Armistice. A second bout of Spanish flu had struck the camp and Manuel was ill for several days. He has no memory of being boarded onto a train for the return trip to England. When the German transport officers recognized Manuel was dangerously ill, he was taken to a hospital in Switzerland, where he made a partial recovery. Manuel did not make it back to England until early 1919, at which point he spent further time convalescing before being repatriated to Newfoundland in May. Manuel moved to Ontario in 1921, where his war wounds required him to spend several years in and out of hospitals, with much of this rehabilitation overseen by the specialists at Christie Street, Toronto.

———

I am certain that any man, regardless of his courage or endurance, who was required to serve in either of the one-sided massacres on the Somme or Passchendaele fronts for one month (or even less), whether he missed being wounded or not, was changed forever. Never again would he be that same individual that he had been prior. His whole perspective of life and death and everything pertaining to each had completely changed. Something deep and vital to his well-being and peace of mind

— something that I have neither the talent nor wisdom to completely define or portray — had been partially or totally destroyed.

Those of our front-line veterans who were fortunate to survive long enough were there to help finish up the war on the morning of November 11th, 1918. They were there to see their most worthy German opponents come forth from their pillboxes, dugouts, and trenches to admit defeat. They were all still very young men in years, but the deep-drawn lines of tension, anxiety, and mental strain belied their age. The fresh and carefree look of youth had long since disappeared; young men had suddenly become old men and had missed all the pleasures of life in between.

The long, frightening weeks, months, and years of misery, torment, and fear was beyond anything that man's nervous system was built to withstand. Yet, after suffering so long while enduring the appalling massacres, slaughters, and butchery, because they had no visible wounds to show the unsympathetic and inexperienced doctors back home, they were classified as 100 percent physically and mentally fit. Without a pension or any financial assistance from the governments who they were sent to fight for in the first place, they were hustled out into a strange, new, unfamiliar world. They were left to wander from factory to factory and from town to town in search of employment in a labour market that was already much overcrowded. To make matters worse, many jobs were drying up now that the need for war supplies had ended.

Owners and managements of factories and industrial plants whose profits had doubled several times over during the war, much of it at government and taxpayers' expense, were also unsympathetic or hesitant about hiring too many ex-front-line veterans. It wasn't that they disliked them, but they were aware of and feared the possible repercussions of "shell shock" (also known as battle fatigue).[1] They learned that sometimes young men, having been discharged from the army, after spending months or years under enemy shellfire and many other terrifying weapons of war, whether they had been wounded or not, were sometimes either physically or mentally incapable of competing for jobs with men whose nervous system had never been subjected to such a horrifying ordeal. In most manufacturing plants containing conveyor belts, assembly lines, etc., if even one man should fall behind with his work, others must stop or slow down until he has caught up. Therefore, we should not condemn such employers for not wanting to hire men who they suspected as being unqualified for the job.

I can distinctly recall an incident that substantiates such reasoning. On my way from Toronto to my home in the Niagara Peninsula one morning in the early twenties, I stopped just west of the city to pick up a young man who was hitching his way to Hamilton. He told me that his friend had phoned him the previous night concerning a job that would be available in one of the huge industrial plants there within a day or two, and he was on his way to apply for it. I noticed that as we approached the city of Hamilton, he removed the small Canadian service badge from the lapel of his old tattered jacket and placed it carefully inside an empty wallet.

When I asked him why he did so, he replied that his friend had warned him that on no account must he let them know at the factory personnel office that he was an ex-serviceman. If he did, his chance of obtaining the job would be hopeless.

When I mentioned that the firm in question would in all probability find out about his deception sooner or later, and when they did, they would likely fire him, "Oh no," he said, "not according to my friend, who has worked there for years." Once he had secured the job and proved to the management's satisfaction that his work and attendance was as good or equal to that of the other employees, the fact that he was a returned veteran would no longer matter and could possibly be to his advantage. His friend had cautioned him to keep quiet about his overseas service only because so many of the veterans previously hired by the firm had proven incapable of producing their full quota of work, while others, owing to their disability, spent far too much time away from the job.

I drove him as far as the plant gate, which was several miles out of my way, and gave him one of the few dollars I had with me to buy himself a meal. A dollar, even less, would buy a hungry man a full-sized meal at that time. I wished him luck and headed back to the highway and down the beautiful scenic Niagara Peninsula toward home.[2] As I drove along through the beautiful blooming peach and cherry orchards, my mind kept pondering over the many and varied changes that had taken place during the five or six short years that had come and gone since Armistice Day. How very different almost everything actually was from what most of us had anticipated and hoped it would be.

All through the four years of mud and blood, or at least from 1915 on, if a young man of military age was seen walking down the street in civilian dress, he was ridiculed. People he had never seen or even heard of before would ask why he was not in uniform. School-age boys and girls were actually encouraged to mock and taunt him. He was scorned and despised by his neighbours, and at many of the street intersections, a young woman would be waiting to step up and present him with a white feather: a symbol of a slacker or coward.

Now less than six years later, a returned front-line veteran was told that he would have a much better chance of procuring a common labourer's job in a factory by hiding his war service badge. The very people whose freedom and wealth he suffered all the miseries and torments of hell to protect would be deceived into believing that he had never served his country.

Many employers felt much the same way about ex-servicemen as they did about ex-convicts. They were afraid to take a chance on either, but not, of course, for the same reason. I don't want to leave the impression that all big business was prejudiced against employing ex-servicemen, but many were, mainly because they felt it was not in their best interest to do so. On the other hand, there were some firms that, in order to help the returned men and their families out during the depression period, hired more of them than they actually needed. Included were two of Canada's leading merchandising firms, which, although they already had a full quota of employees when the war ended, hired many extra returned veterans. Financially, they would have been much better off without the extra employees as many of their stores and warehouses across the country remained overstaffed for several years after.

At war's end, the government might have granted those exhausted and nerve-wracked ex-front-line veterans a year's leave of absence with pay at the Empire's expense. This may have allowed for sufficient time to regain some of their lost morale and self-confidence, time to readjust to civilian life and recuperate from their terrifying months or years of service. Having them all registered as 100 percent physically and mentally fit for hard labour and forced out into a confused world to hunt for work where there was no longer work to be had simply resulted in more suffering and hardships. This could have been averted, and in the long run, both veterans and taxpayers would have benefited.

I am not suggesting that all the men in uniform at the end of the war should have been given a year's holiday with pay. A third or more of them had never reached France prior to the Armistice, and many thousands of those who had were not front-line soldiers. It took approximately three men behind the lines to keep one supplied up front and that does not include the quarter million of Sir Douglas Haig's cavalrymen who sat on their fannies for four long years, waiting for his promised breakthrough.

The soldiers I am referring to were front-line veterans who had escaped being wounded, or [been] wounded seriously enough to be hospitalized for more than a day or so. Believe me, except for the poor boys who were killed or later died of their wounds, those long-enduring, unwounded front-line veterans were the most unfortunate of all front-line troops. Sure, the many thousands of us who were wounded on one or more occasion suffered a certain amount of pain and discomfort for some time, depending on how badly wounded we were. But pain or not, to be back in one of those clean, soft hospital beds in Britain, away from that terrifying battlefront inferno, was glorious heaven compared to the misery and constant fear of death. We rested while many thousands of our unwounded comrades in and around the front-line trenches were still suffering and mentally dying a thousand deaths each and every day.

The cruel war dragged on for more than four long heartbreaking years and cost millions of dollars for each and every day it lasted. Nevertheless, it would be quite safe to predict that if Germany had been sufficiently supplied with food and munitions and was strong enough to have carried on for another four years, the British and Commonwealth governments would have undoubtedly found the hundreds of millions, or billions, necessary to have continued resisting her. Yet, when it was all over, the men at the top of the various governments did not care enough to spend a mere fraction of what another three months of war would have cost toward the re-establishment and future welfare of their burnt-out front-line veterans. For months and years, they had suffered all the misery, horrors, and torments of hell to bring us victory.

———

Manuel again recalls the veteran he picked up hitchhiking near Hamilton, Ontario, in the early 1920s, and the service medal his passenger was determined to keep hidden during his pending employment interview.

———

During the "Hungry Thirties," as they were called, I saw dozens of such medals in the front windows of various pawn shops throughout every city in southwestern Ontario, and in all probability, this was also true in other parts of Canada. Some of those hard-won medals may have been pawned or exchanged by a few poor wretched ex-servicemen who felt that they needed a drink to help them forget their misery far more than they needed the medal itself.

Now that the war was over and the danger past, most governments and big businesses were no longer concerned or cared, but it is to the everlasting shame of the privileged and the ruling class whose property, wealth, and way of life those nerve-wracked, burnt-out ex-front-line veterans suffered and endured all the torments of hell to protect. The majority of those valour medals were neither pawned nor exchanged for drinks or smokes, but parted with only as a last resort — the few miserable pennies given for those very medals to be spent on food for the hungry children of the men who had once been so proud to wear them.

# CONCLUSION

In a long, active life that followed his 1919 RNR discharge, following the Allied forces' demobilization, it is testament to Manuel's drive and physical durability that he succeeds as a hotel owner, husband, and father. He is almost eighty when he decides to return to visit the Beaumont-Hamel battlefield.

———

A few years ago, in 1975, I took a trip back to Britain and the Continent. After spending a couple of weeks in England and Scotland, I went to France, from where I followed as closely as time and transportation would permit what many Newfoundland World War One veterans like to call the "Trail of the Caribou."[1] It actually began in Egypt and the Dardanelles in 1915. Our first big battle in France was the Battle of the Somme, which was really not a battle at all. We suffered more casualties in the first five minutes of leaving our foxholes and trenches there than we did during the entire Gallipoli campaign.

The slaughter began and ended near to what had been, before the continuous week-long bombardment began, a very picturesque country-side village named Beaumont-Hamel. There, for the majority of the boys in our regiment, the Trail of the Caribou ended forever. For the fifty-three who were fortunate enough to come out of it in one piece, and for those of us lucky enough to have survived our wounds to rejoin them later (plus the thousands of newcomers), the trail was again picked up and continued on to such places as Monchy, Langemarck, Cambrai, Sailly-Saillisel, Steenbeck, Combles, and many other battlefronts. Included was Passchendaele, the most tragic name in the history of war, where close to a half million British Empire youths fell without having retaken enough ground to bury them in ...

Passchendaele should have been called Haig's second-biggest stupidity battle; the one on the Somme being his biggest. He never did plan a successful one, and if Marshal Foch had not taken over when he did, we would surely have lost the war, or at least lost what was left of France, Italy, and Belgium.

The town of Albert, six miles away, was the closest I could get to Beaumont-Hamel by bus or train. When I tried to hire a taxi, the cabman wanted $48.50, or the equivalent in French francs, to take me there and back. When I told him what he could do with his taxi, he wanted to bargain, and before I left, he offered to take me there and back for about $10. I would willingly have paid him, plus a generous tip, if he had not tried so hard to make a sucker of me. So, after telling him where he could go and take his taxi with him, I walked all the way there and back. After sitting so much in trains and planes for several days, the twelve-mile walk was just what I needed and I actually enjoyed it.

Personally, I liked the French people, and as a whole, the boys in our regiment got along with them fairly well, much better than the troops from England. However, there is no denying the fact that some of them were covetous and greedy, especially so the small shop owners and innkeepers who frequently charged our boys double the proper rate. The very cheapest French wine for which their own soldiers paid five francs, our boys were charged as much as twelve, seldom if ever less than ten. It was reported that the farmers were paid luxury hotel prices for the use of their stinking old barns we slept in during our so-called rest periods from the front-line trenches. Some of the boys often remarked that in their opinion, we were fighting the wrong people....

The forty-acre memorial park, comprises the ground over which our regiment made such a gallant, though futile, effort to advance. It is very impressive and a fitting tribute to our boys who died there and to all those who died on the many other fronts, including Egypt and the Dardanelles. On one of the highest points in the park, overlooking what was known in 1916 as St. John's Road and the slopes beyond toward what our boys usually referred to as Jerry's front line, the Newfoundland government has erected a magnificent-looking bronze Caribou, which was the regiment's official emblem. It stands on a high mound, rising forty-five or fifty feet above St. John's Road, gazing in the direction of Y Ravine from where, for the lack of proper planning and leadership by our remote generals, our whole regiment was shot down and totally destroyed within minutes of leaving our foxholes and trenches.

Below the majestic looking stag's feet, set in granite rocks projecting from the mound, are bronze plates on which are inscribed not only the names of those who perished on that awesome 1st of July morning, but of whom have no marked graves. One of the first names to catch my eye was Robert Janes, who had been my very dear friend and life-long companion, and as I stood there sixty years later it seemed like only yesterday that he had warned me of the uncut belts of German barbed wire he had seen while out on reconnaissance patrol the night before. Ten minutes or so later, after shaking hands and wishing each other luck, he lay dead just a few feet beyond our own barbed wire; shot through the head. I can still vividly remember a certain sense of relief when I realized that he had died instantly and would not have to suffer hours of torture in the scorching-hot sun before dying of his wounds, as many of the hundreds and thousands who were falling all over no man's land would be compelled to do.

———

It is fitting that Manuel's initial rationale for "telling his story" should provide his conclusion.

———

Generals, colonels, majors, and captains have all written books about the First World War, but in the years that have since come and gone, I have never read or even heard of one that was written by a sergeant, a corporal, or a private, the lowly common front-line foot soldier.

No book represents the infantrymen: the boys who did the actual fighting, endured the hardships, suffered the lice, the rats, the mud, and the blood. Trench-sick, homesick, and sick of the established system responsible for their horrible predicament, in constant mortal fear, they fought, suffered, and died in the blood-drenched Somme and Flanders mud, but few if any cared outside of their own immediate families. I knew of some common soldiers who were fairly well educated, and were in fact much better qualified to lead and command than many of those who did, but they insisted on remaining in the ranks with their comrades and friends.

No doubt there were others quite capable of writing; however, the majority of returned veterans wanted only to forget about their nightmarish experiences in the Somme and Passchendaele infernos. That was precisely the way I felt prior to reading so many books on the subject written by generals and others who had never seen a front-line battlefield; or if they had, it was long after the battle was over.

So many of the descriptions and explanations written by the generals who planned and ordered the very offensive battles that I was unfortunate enough to be a part of were altogether different from my experiences — so much so that if it were not for the many scars that I still carry as a result, I would have grave doubts as to whether I had ever been there at all. Their stories are so different that perhaps it was all just some frightful nightmare that I had undergone — a nightmare whose fearful, tormenting memory still lingers. They write of little bits of stinking, slimy trenches or a few small squares of blood-drenched mud recaptured as if it were an overwhelming victory. Not once do they even bother to mention the appalling loss of life suffered during those many needless and futile offences, nor the fact that in every single instance the Germans never failed (either immediately following, or later when it better served their purpose) to counterattack and take every last scrap of those worthless blood-reddened gains back again....

———

These words, spoken into his newly acquired dictation machine in 1980, are believed to be the first ones Manuel ever spoke about his war experiences. Coloured by more than sixty years of life experience, Manuel appears to have approached his declared Great War reminiscence project with a plan. He devoted obvious energy to his work. It seems likely that Manuel gave at least passing consideration to seeking a wider audience for his Great War account.

Yet such ambitions were never advanced beyond the transcribed pages. Manuel told his story in segments, with his machine recording sixty hours of tape as created over approximately six weeks.[2] His London stenographer dutifully transcribed his words, and she was paid an agreed-upon fee. Grandson David Manuel's 2011 discovery of the original tapes and transcript in an unmarked shoebox buried amongst his late father's effects is suggestive of two possible outcomes.

The first is that Manuel's plan to publish the work was simply overtaken by old age. He died at age eighty-eight — a long life by any standard, and remarkable longevity for one both badly wounded and imprisoned in the harsh slave camp conditions Manuel describes. At the least, one would have expected Manuel to leave instructions for his account to be circulated amongst his family.

The second possibility shoulders its way forward in this Conclusion. Manuel's sole proclamation made to his family regarding what became *A Boy from Botwood* was that he would "tell his story." He did. Perhaps with his memories forever captured by dictation machine and in a proper written record, hearing his own voice tell the story of his younger RNR self was part catharsis and part promise fulfilled. A published version may never have been Manuel's objective. It is our speculation only that Manuel would approve of what has been told of his war in this work.

What is certain from the account Manuel provides of his Great War experience are the powerful ironies and intriguing inconsistencies that abound when Manuel's long post–First World War life is reconstructed.

The passion he expresses for his Newfoundland origins did not prompt Manuel to maintain a close physical connection with his Botwood roots, as far as any of the remaining Manuel family members can recall. He made his 1975 Beaumont-Hamel pilgrimage, but he visited Newfoundland very infrequently — perhaps as few as five times in the sixty years after he left for Ontario in the early 1920s. Manuel expresses deep affection for long-dead RNR comrades, bonds surely made unbreakable and inviolate by terrible shared experience in Gallipoli, the Somme, and Passchendaele. Yet Manuel had no apparent contact with the regiment from his 1919 demobilization until his death. If Manuel kept his service medals, the otherwise coveted "triple" that few RNR men would have been awarded, given the losses the regiment continually sustained until Armistice, they are lost forever. No medals, no wartime keepsakes, and no regiment memorabilia were left behind when Manuel died.

The profound dilemma confronting anyone seeking to retell a story fashioned by its original author with such obvious care sixty years after the fact is one prompted by Manuel's testament. The supporting research verifies beyond any doubt every background fact to which Manuel attests in his *A Boy from Botwood* narrative. His pre-RNR life, enlistment, service, capture, escape, recapture, and postwar life are each verified through a conventional combination of official military records, RNR histories, and family accounts. But Manuel's story will always leave a doubt regarding the complex emotional overlay that he describes in each chapter. How much of what he describes in sixty hours of dictated reminiscences, as originally captured in his four-hundred-page, single-spaced account, is unvarnished by time and life experience? What does he actually remember from the Great War horrors that remains pure and beyond the powerful influence of memory?

How many times did Manuel play and replay these events over in his mind, utter them out loud, or even wonder what others might think? We know from Manuel's own account, and the Christie Street Orthopaedic Hospital records, that he was undergoing further rehabilitation when Erich Maria Remarque visited in the later 1920s. Manuel's description of his Passchendaele capture has close parallels to how Remarque describes his young German soldier narrator's close encounter with death in a shell hole. One cannot help but wonder if Manuel's POW capture narrative borrows something from what became one of best-known First World War works ever published. By the same token, on a muddy, crater-strewn field, where bodies are rotting and plentiful, how Manuel described being wounded and then captured is entirely plausible. His official records confirm both wounds and timing.

But ultimately, does it matter how Manuel remembers events? In his own words, Manuel never seeks to rewrite First World War history. He wants to set the record straight. The Great War was a catastrophic waste of humanity. His contempt for the politicians that put its terrible events in motion is only surpassed by the fury he expresses for the incompetent, unfeeling generals whose strategies were rooted in callous indifference to the common soldiers. It is Manuel's ability to see the best in both comrades and enemies that transcends all battlefield brutality and horror. Jack Crowe, the kind Catholic sister, the Bantam, and the German doctors who helped save his life are each a testament to the good that Manuel sought in a place and time that for him was inherently evil.

Thus, long after death, Manuel remains true to his word. He does not offer a history lesson, or a revisionist First World War account. His words are a cry from the heart: honest and unaffected, resonating and real.

# NOTES

## INTRODUCTION

1. The Newfoundland Regiment was given the "Royal" prefix by King George V on December 17, 1917, in recognition of the Regiment's notable contributions to the Allied war effort. We use "Royal Newfoundland Regiment/RNR" throughout this work for simplicity and consistency.

2. This "triple" is mentioned in various RNR accounts, with examples on display at the Royal Newfoundland Regimental Museum, St. John's.

3. Interestingly, detailed inquiries made directly through official Canadian Veterans Affairs (VA) channels (November 2014) and later kind assistance provided by the RNR (St. John's Newfoundland, January 2015) indirectly confirms this family account. The official Manuel file maintained by VA is incomplete; portions that would otherwise be expected in a veteran file where the subject received ongoing medical treatment (Manuel was treated at various times between 1919 and 1932 at Christie Street Orthopaedic Hospital, Toronto) are missing. This fact is consistent with Manuel being involved in a 1980-era VA dispute, with documents being removed at that time for review — and never returned to the file.

4. The overlay between later Manuel impressions and actual First World War experience is exemplified here. Manuel met Remarque in 1929 at

the Christie Street Orthopaedic Hospital, Toronto, while Manuel was undergoing follow-up treatment for his war injuries — he undoubtedly read *All Quiet on the Western Front* numerous times.

5.  In the raw manuscript from which this book has been created, Manuel's first words were "I am going to tell my story." This phrase is highlighted here accordingly.

## CHAPTER 1: BOTWOOD, 1908

1.  From the various family sources, Manuel was fourteen years old at this time (summer 1910).

2.  Equal to 112 pounds; Manuel describes the quintal as the popular measure used by fishermen "prior to Confederation." As with any Newfoundlander of Manuel's era, Confederation meant the 1949 Newfoundland entry, not Canada's 1867 founding.

3.  This is one of several points in his narrative where Manuel conflates Newfoundland's First World War British colony status with post-1949 Newfoundland's status as a Canadian province, and part of the "nation."

4.  It is an intriguing genealogical feature of Manuel's account that despite his very large family, he had little contact with various siblings, cousins, and other relatives after he relocated to Ontario after 1921. Whenever family is mentioned in the narrative, Manuel speaks with apparent affection, yet actual contact seems very limited.

## CHAPTER 2: ST. JOHN'S, AUGUST 1914

1.  The "Royal" designation was award to the regiment by King George V in September 1917, in recognition of the regiment's valour displayed during various Ypres engagements. The Third Battle of Ypres occurred at Passchendaele, where Manuel was first taken prisoner.

2.  There are numerous excellent treatments of this part of the RNR story, including Richard Cramm's *The First 500*, initially published in 1921, and, more recently, Edward Roberts' work *Sydney Frost: A Blue Puttee at War*, 2014.

3.  Partial amputation of his left foot, the injury Manuel sustained at the hands of the POW slave camp *Field Webel* on his POW recapture in late 1917.

4. Stobs Camp (1903–59), located near Hawick village in the Scottish Borders country, was an important British Army training base. During the First World War the RNR recruits were housed at Acreknowe Camp, approximately 500 metres from the main Stobs facility.

## CHAPTER 3: GALLIPOLI, 1915

1. Shallow-bottomed boats used for carrying supplies to the beach positions.

2. Moudros (commonly spelled *Mudros* in the BEF and RNR accounts) is a Greek town and harbour used by the Allies as a support base during the Dardanelles campaign.

3. A grenade developed in 1915 by William Mills, a British engineer. The bomb's novel feature was its central spring-loaded firing pin and spring-loaded lever. Once thrown, the lever released the striker, igniting a four-second time fuse that allowed the thrower to take cover prior to explosion. The bomb's cast-iron casing would shatter; its metal fragments were often deadly at close range.

4. Beaches held by the Australian and New Zealand forces (ANZAC).

5. The RNR location.

6. It is uncertain where Manuel may have read this specific Gallipoli evacuation account. The RNR role played in the evacuation is well documented, and consistent with the sentiment Manuel expressed here; see, for example, Colonel G.W.L. Nicholson, *The Fighting Newfoundlander*, 2nd Revised edition (Montreal: McGill-Queen's University Press, 2006), 188, 227.

7. General Otto Liman von Sanders (1855–1929) is widely regarded as having transforming the Ottoman army into an efficient fighting unit by the First World War's commencement.

8. The precise source that Manuel references here is unknown. He may have summarized a comment made in one of the many First World War histories he later read that contributed to his opinions expressed throughout his writings.

9. General Sir Ian Hamilton, *Gallipoli Diary* (London: Edward Arnold, 1920), available online, https://ia802702.us.archive.org/25/items/gallipolidiary02hamiuoft/gallipolidiary02hamiuoft.pdf.

## CHAPTER 4: BEAUMONT-HAMEL, JULY 1916

1. Farrar-Hockley (1924–2006) was a noted British senior officer and military historian.

2. Anthony Heritage Farrar-Hockley *The Somme* (London: Pan Books, 1964), 224.

3. As with note 18, it is likely that Manuel read a German officer's description of Beaumont-Hamel without providing a verbatim quote. Similar accounts appear at numerous German military sources, including the diaries of various 119th Infantry Regiment soldiers, assembled by German military expert Rolf Schafer, "Hawthorn Ridge Mine — The German experience, Somme, 1st of July 1916" *Gott mit uns! German Military History 1848–1945* (2016), available online, https://gottmituns.net.

4. The term *whiz-bang* was originally applied by Allied troops to the noise made by shells fired from German 77mm field guns; it later was used in connection with all light artillery field guns.

## CHAPTER 5: ENGLAND, AUTUMN 1916

1. Also known as the Battle of Langemarck, August 16–18, 1917, near Ypres, in Belgium.

## CHAPTER 6: PASSCHENDAELE, AUGUST 1917

1. An excellent study of First World War Canadian media coverage and its thinly veiled propaganda effects is provided in Jeffrey A. Keshen and Serge Marc Durflinger, *War and Society in Post-Confederation Canada* (Toronto: Nelson Education, 2006).

2. General Friedrich Karl "Fritz" von Lossberg (1868–1942), renowned German strategist and military planner.

3. An early field telephone developed for combat and front-line communications.

4. Manuel underwent various surgeries at different times for at least ten years after his 1919 demobilization. His longest hospital stays were at Toronto's Christie Street Orthopaedic Hospital, where he underwent therapy and at least one surgery on the elbow badly damaged at Beaumont-Hamel.

5. "The Lord is my shepherd; I shall not want. He maketh me to lie down

in green pastures: he leadeth me beside the still waters. He restoreth my soul: he leadeth me in the paths of righteousness for his name's sake." Manuel makes various Biblical references throughout his raw manuscript, a fact attributable to his family's poverty, the Bible would have provided the most frequent reading material.

6. Located in eastern Flanders (Belgium).

7. "English pigs."

8. Located in the Ardennes region, northeastern France.

9. Manuel uses the phrase *Field Webel*; his usage is maintained here. *Feldwebel* is a non-commissioned officer rank, the German equivalent of a British or RNR company sergeant-major.

10. A type of beetroot, sometimes boiled and eaten as a vegetable; more commonly used as animal food.

11. Manuel's official file suggests he may have weighed as little as ninety-five pounds on his late-1917 German recapture; he enlisted at 145 pounds in 1914.

12. The key German defensive fortifications (known to the Germans as the "Siegfried Line") as constructed from Arras, near Vimy Ridge, in northeastern France, to Laffaux, near Soissons on the Aisne River.

13. The well-known central-London park, best known for its Speaker's Corner, where open-air public speaking and often robust debates of political issues have been a feature for over two hundred years.

14. This "super-man" reference is likely a product of Manuel's extensive post–First World War reading. German and related Aryan race supremacy theories had been published prior to the First World War, but these became very well known in the Second World War era, after the rise of Adolf Hitler and German Nazism.

15. Erich Maria Remarque.

16. The traditional Cockney definition that Manuel would have known, namely those born within earshot the bells of St. Mary-le-Bow Church, London, famously rebuilt by Sir Christopher Wren after the Great Fire of 1666.

## CHAPTER 7: PRISONER OF WAR, OCTOBER 1917

1. Private George Brown, Australia (ANZACS), Manuel's closest escape-planning POW.

## CHAPTER 8: BAVARIA, JANUARY 1918

1.  The offensive term (French origin) used to describe Germans during the First World War.
2.  A town located in the Upper Palatinate, Bavaria, approximately one hundred kilometres north of Munich, and close to the modern-day German border with the Czech Republic.
3.  General Erich Ludendorf (1865–1937) was responsible for leading a general offensive on the Western Front with the object of smashing the Anglo-French armies and forcing a decision in Europe before the Americans arrived in force. But he had overestimated the strength of the German armies; the offensive failed.
4.  Famous in literary history as the setting for Mary Shelley's novel *Frankenstein*, Ingolstadt is located in central Bavaria on the River Danube.
5.  In modern medicine, this very dangerous condition is known as the "refeeding syndrome." Death may result if the starved patient ingests too much food too quickly, as their damaged bodies cannot properly process (metabolize) proteins and nutrients.
6.  Royal Army Medical Corp.
7.  Manuel operated a hotel for many years in Windsor, Ontario, with the Detroit River his reference here.
8.  John Russel "Jack" Crowe (1895–1954), was sometimes referred to in post–First World War Ontario reports as "Owen Sound's legless veteran." In a 2014 Owen Sound media account, on his 1919 repatriation Crowe told his family that after his POW capture the German soldiers took him to hospital and saved his life (Scott Dunn, "War Medals Return, Family Thrilled," *Owen Sound Times*, April 10, 2014, available online, www.owensoundsuntimes.com/2014/04/10/war-medals-return-family-thrilled.
9.  The modern Parry Sound, Ontario, district, eastern Lake Huron.
10. In 1924, as confirmed by the Christie Street Hospital records, and those maintained by Veterans Affairs Canada.
11. Manuel may be describing Ruhleben, the oldest of the German POW camps, located near Berlin.
12. The Battle of Courcelette was part of the later Somme advance attempted by the British forces near Amiens between September 15

and September 22. Courcelette is significant as the first time British tanks were deployed in combat. The Canadian Corps (as formed from the Canadian Expeditionary Force) played a prominent role at Courcelette. Total Allied casualties were almost 30,000, with 20,000 for the German forces.

13. Manuel is describing the famous "Flag Debate," 1965.

14. The U.S. officially entered the war in April 1917; the first American units were deployed in France during the Battle of Cambrai, November 1917, but significant U.S. influence was not felt until spring 1918; see (among many excellent sources) David R Woodward, *The American Army and the First World War* (Cambridge University Press, 2014).

15. The name attached to these BEF veterans, from the Battle of Mons 1914. They are honoured (amongst many locations) at Westminster Abbey, London.

16. The 1918 Spanish flu pandemic would eventually contribute to the deaths of an estimated fifty to a hundred million people worldwide by 1920. In many cases, the influenza onset weakened the afflicted person's immune system; death from pneumonia was a common outcome.

## CHAPTER 9: ARMISTICE, NOVEMBER 1918

1. Now a condition generally described as PTSD (post-traumatic stress disorder).

2. For Manuel, home was now Windsor, Ontario.

## CONCLUSION

1. Beaumont-Hamel is maintained as a national park by the Canadian government.

2. As determined from the manner in which the tapes were stored and labelled.

# INDEX

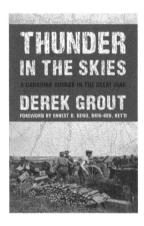

Thunder in the Skies
Derek Grout

What was it like to be a field gunner in the Great War?

Drawing on the unpublished letters and diary of field gunner Lt. Bert Sargent and his fellow soldiers, Thunder in the Skies takes the reader from enlistment in late 1914, through training camp, to the Somme, Vimy Ridge, Passchendaele, the Hundred Days Offensive, and home again with peace.

Posted just behind the front lines, Sargent and field gunners like him spent gruelling months supporting the infantry in the trenches. Theirs was a very different war, as dangerous or more at times as the one on the front lines. As an ordinary Canadian writing letters home to ordinary people, Sargent gives a wrenching, insightful account of a tight-knit band of soldiers swept up in some of the most important battles of the war that shaped the twentieth century.

Thunder in the Skies details the daily life of artillerymen fighting in the First World War in a way no other book has before.

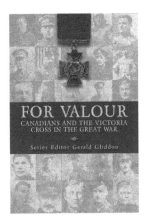

For Valour
Gerald Gliddon

As Canada came into its own as a nation during the First World War, proving itself capable of standing alongside Britain on the world stage, scores of Canadians were awarded the Commonwealth's highest award for pre-eminent acts of valour, self-sacrifice, or extreme devotion to duty, the Victoria Cross. For Valour details every Canadian VC recipient from the First World War. These men, ordinary servicemen from widely differing social backgrounds, acted with valour above and beyond the call of duty. Their stories and experiences offer a fresh perspective on the "war to end all wars."

Series editor Gerald Gliddon and contributors Stephen Snelling and Peter F. Batchelor examine the men and the dramatic events that led to the granting of this most prized of medals. Each of the men's stories is different, but they all have one thing in common — acts of extraordinary bravery under fire.

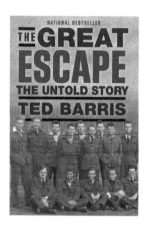

The Great Escape
Ted Barris

2014 Libris Award — Joint Winner, Non-Fiction Book of the Year

On the night of March 24, 1944, eighty airmen crawled through a 400-foot-long tunnel, code-named "Harry," and dashed from Stalag Luft III, the infamous WWII German POW camp. It became known as The Great Escape. The breakout had taken a year to plan, involved 2,000 POWs, and prompted a massive manhunt across occupied Europe. All but three escapees were recaptured, and on Hitler's orders, fifty were murdered.

Bestselling author Ted Barris revisits the story made famous by the 1963 movie. But he recounts this battle of wits and determination through the voices of those involved. Drawing on the experiences of forty years of experience as a journalist, broadcaster, and historian, Barris assembles original interviews, memoirs, letters, diaries, and personal photos to reconstruct the Great Escape's untold story.

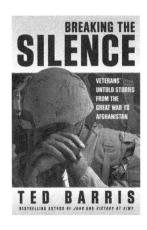

Breaking the Silence
Ted Barris

"Never talked about it."

That's what most people say when they're asked if the veteran in the family ever shared wartime experiences. Describing combat, imprisonment or lost comrades from the World Wars, the Korea War, or even Afghanistan is reserved for Remembrance Day or the Legion lounge. Nobody was ever supposed to see them get emotional, show their vulnerability. Nobody was ever to know the hell of their war.

About twenty-five years ago, Ted Barris began breaking through the silence. Because of his unique interviewing skills, he found that veterans would talk to him, set the record straight and put a face on the service and sacrifice of men and women in uniform. As a result of his work on fifteen previous books, Barris has earned a reputation of trust among Canada's veterans. Indeed, over the years, nearly 3,000 of them have shared their memories, all offering original material for his books.

Among other revelations in *Breaking the Silence*, veterans of the Great War reflect on an extraordinary first Armistice in 1918; decorated Second World War fighter pilots talk about their thirst for blood in the sky; Canadian POWs explain how they survived Chinese attempts to brainwash them during the Korean War; and soldiers with the Afghanistan mission talk about the horrors of the "friendly fire" incident near Kandahar.

*Breaking the Silence* is a ground-breaking book that goes to the heart of veterans' wartime experiences.

# WW I

| | Dead | Wounded |
|---|---|---|
| G. B. | 702,000 | 1,670,000 |
| India ~~Aust~~ | 64,000 | 67,000 |
| Canada | 56,700 | 150,000 |
| New Z | 16,700 | 41,300 |
| S. Africa | 7,000 | 12,000 |
| New foundland | 1,200 | 2,200 |
| Aust | 59,300 | 152,000 |